P9-DHZ-318

HJ 2051 .U7 2013

The US deficit

NEW ENGLAND INSTITUTE OF TECHNOLOGY
LIBRARY

The US Deficit

Other Books of Related Interest:

At Issue Series
Are Executives Paid Too Much?
Health Care Legislation

Current Controversies Series
Politics and the Media
The Tea Party Movement

Global Viewpoints Series
Capitalism

Opposing Viewpoints Series
Democracy
Election Spending
The Minimum Wage
Poverty
The U.S. Census
Welfare

"Congress shall make no law . . . abridging the freedom of speech, or of the press."

First Amendment to the US Constitution

The basic foundation of our democracy is the First Amendment guarantee of freedom of expression. The Opposing Viewpoints series is dedicated to the concept of this basic freedom and the idea that it is more important to practice it than to enshrine it.

The US Deficit

Kathy Jennings and Lynn M. Zott, Book Editors

GREENHAVEN PRESS
A part of Gale, Cengage Learning

NEW ENGLAND INSTITUTE OF TECHNOLOGY
LIBRARY

GALE
CENGAGE Learning·

Detroit • New York • San Francisco • New Haven, Conn • Waterville, Maine • London

2\13   # 783171217

GALE
CENGAGE Learning·

Elizabeth Des Chenes, *Director, Publishing Solutions*

© 2013 Greenhaven Press, a part of Gale, Cengage Learning.

Gale and Greenhaven Press are registered trademarks used herein under license.

For more information, contact:
Greenhaven Press
27500 Drake Rd.
Farmington Hills, MI 48331-3535
Or you can visit our Internet site at gale.cengage.com

ALL RIGHTS RESERVED.
No part of this work covered by the copyright herein may be reproduced, transmitted, stored, or used in any form or by any means graphic, electronic, or mechanical, including but not limited to photocopying, recording, scanning, digitizing, taping, Web distribution, information networks, or information storage and retrieval systems, except as permitted under Section 107 or 108 of the 1976 United States Copyright Act, without the prior written permission of the publisher.

For product information and technology assistance, contact us at

Gale Customer Support, 1-800-877-4253
For permission to use material from this text or product, submit all requests online at
www.cengage.com/permissions

Further permissions questions can be emailed to permissionrequest@cengage.com

Articles in Greenhaven Press anthologies are often edited for length to meet page requirements. In addition, original titles of these works are changed to clearly present the main thesis and to explicitly indicate the author's opinion. Every effort is made to ensure that Greenhaven Press accurately reflects the original intent of the authors. Every effort has been made to trace the owners of copyrighted material.

Cover Image copyright © Jim Barber/Shutterstock.com.

LIBRARY OF CONGRESS CATALOGING-IN-PUBLICATION DATA

The US deficit / Kathy Jennings and Lynn M. Zott, book editors.
    p. cm. -- (Opposing viewpoints)
    Includes bibliographical references and index.
    978-0-7377-6050-7 (hardcover) -- ISBN 978-0-7377-6051-4 (pbk.)
    1. Budget deficits--United States. 2. Government spending policy--United States.
    3. Taxation--United States. 4. United States--Economic policy--2009- I. Jennings,
    Kathy. II. Zott, Lynn M. (Lynn Marie), 1969-
    HJ2051.U7 2012
    339.5'230973--dc23
                                                                    2012023738

Printed in the United States of America
1 2 3 4 5 6 7 16 15 14 13 12

Contents

Chapter 3: Will Cuts to Entitlement Programs Reduce the Deficit?

Chapter 4: Should Defense Spending Be Cut to Reduce the Deficit?

Why Consider Opposing Viewpoints?

> *"The only way in which a human being can make some approach to knowing the whole of a subject is by hearing what can be said about it by persons of every variety of opinion and studying all modes in which it can be looked at by every character of mind. No wise man ever acquired his wisdom in any mode but this."*
>
> John Stuart Mill

In our media-intensive culture it is not difficult to find differing opinions. Thousands of newspapers and magazines and dozens of radio and television talk shows resound with differing points of view. The difficulty lies in deciding which opinion to agree with and which "experts" seem the most credible. The more inundated we become with differing opinions and claims, the more essential it is to hone critical reading and thinking skills to evaluate these ideas. Opposing Viewpoints books address this problem directly by presenting stimulating debates that can be used to enhance and teach these skills. The varied opinions contained in each book examine many different aspects of a single issue. While examining these conveniently edited opposing views, readers can develop critical thinking skills such as the ability to compare and contrast authors' credibility, facts, argumentation styles, use of persuasive techniques, and other stylistic tools. In short, the Opposing Viewpoints Series is an ideal way to attain the higher-level thinking and reading skills so essential in a culture of diverse and contradictory opinions.

In addition to providing a tool for critical thinking, Opposing Viewpoints books challenge readers to question their own strongly held opinions and assumptions. Most people form their opinions on the basis of upbringing, peer pressure, and personal, cultural, or professional bias. By reading carefully balanced opposing views, readers must directly confront new ideas as well as the opinions of those with whom they disagree. This is not to argue simplistically that everyone who reads opposing views will—or should—change his or her opinion. Instead, the series enhances readers' understanding of their own views by encouraging confrontation with opposing ideas. Careful examination of others' views can lead to the readers' understanding of the logical inconsistencies in their own opinions, perspective on why they hold an opinion, and the consideration of the possibility that their opinion requires further evaluation.

Evaluating Other Opinions

To ensure that this type of examination occurs, Opposing Viewpoints books present all types of opinions. Prominent spokespeople on different sides of each issue as well as well-known professionals from many disciplines challenge the reader. An additional goal of the series is to provide a forum for other, less known, or even unpopular viewpoints. The opinion of an ordinary person who has had to make the decision to cut off life support from a terminally ill relative, for example, may be just as valuable and provide just as much insight as a medical ethicist's professional opinion. The editors have two additional purposes in including these less known views. One, the editors encourage readers to respect others' opinions—even when not enhanced by professional credibility. It is only by reading or listening to and objectively evaluating others' ideas that one can determine whether they are worthy of consideration. Two, the inclusion of such viewpoints encourages the important critical thinking skill of objectively evaluating an author's credentials and bias. This evaluation will illuminate an author's reasons for taking a particular stance on an issue and will aid in readers' evaluation of the author's ideas.

It is our hope that these books will give readers a deeper understanding of the issues debated and an appreciation of the complexity of even seemingly simple issues when good and honest people disagree. This awareness is particularly important in a democratic society such as ours in which people enter into public debate to determine the common good. Those with whom one disagrees should not be regarded as enemies but rather as people whose views deserve careful examination and may shed light on one's own.

Thomas Jefferson once said that "difference of opinion leads to inquiry, and inquiry to truth." Jefferson, a broadly educated man, argued that "if a nation expects to be ignorant and free . . . it expects what never was and never will be." As individuals and as a nation, it is imperative that we consider the opinions of others and examine them with skill and discernment. The Opposing Viewpoints series is intended to help readers achieve this goal.

David L. Bender and Bruno Leone,
Founders

Introduction

> *"The debate right now isn't about whether we need to make tough choices. Democrats and Republicans agree on the amount of deficit reduction we need. The debate is about how it should be done. . . . We all want a government that lives within its means, but there are still things we need to pay for as a country—things like new roads and bridges; weather satellites and food inspection; services to veterans and medical research."*
>
> *—President Barack Obama, speech delivered on July 25, 2011*

Shortly after the Joint Select Committee on Deficit Reduction was formed by the federal legislature in August 2011, the media began to refer to it as the Super Committee, a reflection of the broad powers it would have.

The bipartisan, twelve-member committee was given the responsibility of finding ways to cut the federal budget by $1.2 trillion through 2021. Its recommendations could include budget cuts and tax increases as it deemed necessary. The committee began work and held its first public hearing on September 13, 2011, in Washington, DC. It looked at the federal workforce in terms of size, number of employees, pay and benefits and examined whether there were possible savings in extending the existing freeze on pay raises. It debated whether there should be cuts to Medicare, Medicaid, and Social Security. It looked at whether taxes on the nation's wealthiest citizens should be raised. Cuts in military spending were proposed. The committee reached a rough agreement, but when it came to the details they could not come to an accord.

In the end, the committee released this statement: "Despite our inability to bridge the committee's significant differences, we end this process united in our belief that the nation's fiscal crisis must be addressed and that we cannot leave it for the next generation to solve. We remain hopeful that Congress can build on this committee's work and can find a way to tackle this issue in a way that works for the American people and our economy. We are deeply disappointed that we have been unable to come to a bipartisan deficit reduction agreement."

Committee members were not the only ones disappointed that no agreement was reached. Poll numbers showed 44 percent of American voters blamed Republicans for the committee's failure. President Obama and the Democrats were blamed by 38 percent. Despite those numbers, the same poll showed that many of those responding—49 percent—were more sympathetic to the Republican position that the deficit could be closed through budget cuts. The Democratic plan for budget cuts, along with some tax increases, was supported by 39 percent of respondents. Since the committee could reach no agreement, automatic budget cuts were scheduled to take place. The cuts total $1.2 trillion and are set to take effect in 2013, continuing for nine years. Many expect Congress will act before those cuts are implemented. The automatic cuts do not touch Social Security, Medicaid, or many other programs that provide services to low-income Americans. Any Medicare cuts would affect payments to providers, not beneficiaries. In other parts of the federal budget, the automatic cuts would affect defense and nondefense programs equally.

The failure of the budget reduction committee to reach an agreement is the second attempt since President Barack Obama's administration took office to reach an agreement that both political parties could accept. The National Commission on Fiscal Responsibility and Reform was created in February 2010 to find ways to reduce the nation's debt. The commission's work, better known as the Bowles-Simpson plan, named after its chairmen Erskine Bowles and Alan K. Simpson, was supported by eleven of its eighteen members. However, it needed fourteen supporters for the proposal to be sent to Congress for action.

When President Obama established the commission, he told the body made up of elected officials and private citizens that "everything has to be on the table." A draft plan released by the commission showed it was considering eliminating $1 trillion in tax breaks for individuals and corporations. Its proposal was that $3 in cuts to government services, defense, and entitlement programs would be made for every $1 of new tax revenue gained by closing tax loopholes.

The draft plan would have made Social Security solvent for seventy-five years through increased payroll taxes for wealthy individuals and would have raised the age at which people become eligible for benefits to sixty-nine. Military spending would have had a $100 billion budget cut. Altogether, the commission expected its plan to reduce deficit spending by $4 trillion over ten years.

The commission met for nine months and released a plan that many budget reform groups liked, but that was largely ignored by the president and congressional leaders. The Obama administration did not support the deep cuts proposed to Social Security and viewed them as arbitrary to its plan to set a spending limit. In Congress, Republicans objected to recommended tax increases, and Democrats challenged proposed cuts to Social Security and health care expenditures. Though the Bowles-Simpson plan never made its way to Congress, many of the solutions it proposed continue to be debated as efforts to control government spending proceed.

The federal budget is important not only as a result of its influence on the national economy but also because of what it represents symbolically. How the federal budget is spent is expected to reflect the values and priorities of the majority of Americans. It is common to hear that federal finances are a mess and spending is out of control, and the following viewpoints regarding the US budget deficit clearly illustrate that there is little to no agreement over how to correct the situation. The authors of the viewpoints in *Opposing Viewpoints: The US Deficit* explore the vastly differing approaches to the various causes and proposed solutions to the budget deficit in the following chapters: What Are Some Key Issues in the Debate over the Deficit?, What Role Should Taxes Play in Deficit Reduction?, Will Cuts to Entitlement Programs Reduce the Deficit?, and Should Defense Spending Be Cut to Reduce the Deficit? The authors examine taxation; military spending; and Medicare, Medicaid, and Social Security programs as they relate to the US budget deficit.

OPPOSING
VIEWPOINTS®
SERIES

CHAPTER 1

What Are Some Key Issues in the Debate over the Deficit?

Chapter Preface

The US federal budget is made up of revenues and expenditures. Taxes and fees make up the revenues. Those are spent on federal programs, from inspection of food to construction of highways to arming the military. A deficit occurs when the total spent exceeds the amount brought in during a given year. The government then borrows money to make up the difference.

The US deficit hit $1.3 trillion in 2011, topping $1 trillion for the third year in a row. One way to measure the deficit is to compare it to the total size of the economy. For example, in 2009 total economic output—known as the gross domestic product, or GDP—was estimated to be worth about $14.1 trillion, and the deficit was about 11.2 percent of that. Economists and politicians differ on what deficit percentage is acceptable and at what point running deficits stifle the economy. Some point out that since 1930 the US government has run a deficit in all but thirteen years. Others suggest the current levels of spending are unprecedented, so comparisons to past years are not relevant.

When it comes to the federal budget, there is a difference between debt and deficit. When the government spends more than it collects in revenue and runs a deficit, it needs to make up the difference through borrowing. The total amount borrowed is the national debt. The debt is the amount of money the US government owes creditors from whom it has borrowed to cover the deficit. The government borrows money by issuing treasury bills, notes, and bonds. It also borrows money from within the government, such as money from the Social Security Trust Fund.

How the deficit influences the US economy is one issue discussed in the following chapter of *Opposing Viewpoints: The US Deficit*. Other topics examined are the relationship between the deficit and job growth, whether deficits should be a matter of concern, and how economic policy and the deficit are connected.

| "You can't really fix the economy or the job picture if you don't also fix the country's long-term debt problem. And make no mistake, our federal debt and the costs of servicing it are a major piece of the deficit problem."

Deficit Reduction Is Crucial to Strengthen the US Economy

Carla Fried

Carla Fried is a personal finance and business writer who contributes to a number of publications, including the New York Times *and* Money *magazine. In the following viewpoint, Fried says that although most Americans want the US Congress to focus on creating jobs, there are key reasons it is important that the nation's debt must be resolved. Very soon, Fried insists, the US government runs the risk of having more debt than economic growth, a circumstance that is unsustainable. If the US debt problem is not resolved quickly, Fried concludes, the problem will worsen and endanger the US economy and national security.*

Carla Fried, "Four Critical Reasons Why You Should Care About the Budget Deficit," *CBS Moneywatch*, November 17, 2010. http://www.cbsnews.com/8301-505123_162-41141619/4-critical-reasons-why-you-should-care-about-the-budget-deficit/?tag=mwuser. Copyright © 2010, CBS News. All rights reserved. Reproduced by permission.

As you read, consider the following questions:

1. What does Fried say are the long-term economic consequences of owing $1 trillion in interest payments?

2. What does Fried contend would be the results if foreign countries that currently own about half of the United States' federal debt insist on being paid?

3. What revenue increase would the United States need to solve its debt crisis if it has until 2020 to tackle the problem, according to Fried?

The latest deficit reduction plan, this one proposed by the Bipartisan Policy Center (BPC), calls for instituting a 6.5 percent "national consumption" tax (essentially, a sales tax) and suspending the Social Security payroll tax in 2011 in order to spur economic growth. These are two distinctive elements that didn't make it into last week's [in November 2010] Bowles-Simpson deficit reduction proposal [referring to recommendations by the National Commission on Fiscal Responsibility and Reform].

If all this nitty-gritty talk about ways to reduce the budget deficit makes your eyes glaze over, you're not alone. In a CBS News poll released last week, just 4 percent of Americans surveyed said the budget deficit should be the main focus of the new Congress come January. By comparison, 56 percent said jobs and the economy should be at the top of Congress's 2011 To Do list.

With unemployment stuck near 10 percent and a molasses-slow recovery holding back job and salary growth, it certainly makes sense that Americans are channeling [Democratic political strategist James] Carville's famous "It's the Economy, Stupid" mantra.

What Is Getting Lost in the Deficit Debate

But what's getting lost in the mix here is that you can't really fix the economy or the job picture if you don't also fix the country's long-term debt problem. And make no mistake, our federal debt and the costs of servicing it are a major piece of the deficit problem. In fact, the 6.5 percent national sales tax proposed by the BPC was specifically labeled a "debt-reduction sales tax."

Below are four reasons you really, truly want the [President Barack] Obama administration and Congress to get their acts together and come up with a long-term plan to tackle our crushing debt. How we do it is what should be debated. But to not have that debate today and to just kick the proverbial can down the road would make today's economic woes seem minor in comparison. Here's why we all need Washington to tackle our massive debt load:

1. *"We are running the risk of debt growing larger than the economy."* Those are the exact words uttered by former senator and BPC member Tom Daschle when he kicked off the release of the BPC deficit reduction plan. That's not some dramatic political posturing; it's just the cold and sobering facts.

The standard way to measure the impact of our federal debt is to look at it relative to the country's gross domestic product (GDP). Before the financial crisis, our federal debt as a percentage of GDP was motoring along at 40 percent, not too much worse than the long-term average of 36 percent. This year, however, the Congressional Budget Office (CBO) projects our debt will reach 62 percent of GDP. If we just sit on our hands and do nothing, the CBO predicts that our debt will hit 90 percent of GDP by 2020, and eventually surpass total economic output in 2025. By 2037, the debt would exceed 200 percent of GDP.

The BPC deficit reduction plan lays out the lovely fact that in 2020, the federal government will owe $1 trillion in interest payments on our federal debt; that represents 17 percent of all our spending. "Viewed another way, the federal government will have to allocate about half of all income tax receipts to pay interest, and interest payments will exceed the size of the defense budget," is how the BPC puts it. . . . Other than Medicare and Medicaid (that's a topic for another day), our national debt will be the fastest-growing problem.

Debt Poses Grave Economic and National Security Risks

2. Once federal debt exceeds 90 percent of GDP, history tells us growth slows dramatically. Ken Rogoff and Carmen Reinhart are former IMF [International Monetary Fund] honchos and well-respected economic academics who wrote 2009's influential *This Time Is Different* that chronicles hundreds of years of global financial crises. The duo recently released a study that found that once a developed country's debt exceeds 90 percent of GDP, its economic growth takes a serious hit. (Just a reminder: We're currently scheduled to hit that figure by 2020.) In their study, "Growth in a Time of Debt," they write that:

> "Over the past two centuries, debt in excess of 90 percent [of GDP] has typically been associated with [average] growth of 1.7 percent, versus 3.7 percent when debt is low (under 30 percent of GDP)."

If you want to see our economy grow at a stronger pace, you should be rooting for Washington to figure out a way to reduce our debt. The BPC plan aims to keep the long-term ratio at its current 60 percent level.

3. High debt loads make it more expensive to borrow and weaken our global position. The CBO recently weighed in on the long-term impact of carrying around a whole lot of debt, saying that "if debt continued to rise rapidly relative to GDP, investors at some point would begin to doubt the government's willingness to pay interest on that debt."

Now no one is suggesting the U.S. would default on its debt; that's not what's at play here. The more pressing problem is that those investors—China, Japan, and the other foreign countries that currently own about half of our federal debt—would insist on getting paid more interest to keep financing our debt. That's exactly what is happening in Europe right now; Ireland's bond yields have jumped amid its ongoing debt crisis and just yesterday Portugal saw the yield on a new 1-year government bond pop up to 4.8 percent, compared to 3.3 percent on an offering from two weeks ago.

If we end up needing to lift our interest rates well beyond their historic norms, that's nothing but bad news for our economy and for jobs. At Wednesday's BPC press conference, former senator Pete Domenici, co-head of the group's debt reduction task force, repeatedly referred to the debt as our nation's "quiet killer" and referenced an earlier statement from Joint Chiefs of Staff Chairman Mike Mullen that our nation's debt is "the single biggest threat to our national security."

4. *Kicking the deficit can down the road makes it even worse.* There is no question Washington has an overabundance of issues to juggle right now, and in the prioritizing process it's always natural to put your short-term worries up top and push the longer-term problems far down the To Do list. But running away from our debt and deficit problem is just going to make the eventual solution even more costly to all of us.

The [Government] Accountability Office (GAO) has a handy calculation that measures how much we would need to increase taxes and reduce spending to bring our revenue in line with spending (not just money spent on servicing our debt, but all our spending). In its latest "fiscal gap" calculation, the GAO estimates that if we attacked the problem today, it would take either a 52 percent increase in revenue (i.e., taxes), or a 35 percent decrease in non-interest-related spending. But if we wait until 2020 to tackle the problem, we'd need either a 62 percent increase in revenues, or a 40 percent cut in spending. That's quite an expensive trade-off for doing nothing today. And as the GAO points out, putting off action also raises the pain factor:

"The longer action to deal with the nation's long-term fiscal outlook is delayed, the greater the risk that the eventual changes will be disruptive and destabilizing."

There are no easy choices here. But to make no choice is just irresponsible. If you care about the economy and jobs in 2011, you need to be just as concerned with what Washington does—sooner rather than later—to deal with our federal debt and deficit. The issues are attached at the hip.

| "Deficit reduction is important. But it is a means to an end—not an end in itself."

Deficit Reduction Will Not Strengthen the US Economy

Joseph E. Stiglitz

Joseph E. Stiglitz was chief economist of the World Bank from 1997 to 2000 and chairman of the Council of Economic Advisers under President Bill Clinton from 1995 to 1997. In the following viewpoint, he presents the case that deficit reduction, if not done responsibly, can weaken the American economy. Stiglitz outlines why he did not join his fellow economists in signing a letter in support of the recommendations of the National Commission on Fiscal Responsibility and Reform, also known as the Bowles-Simpson deficit reduction plan. The Bowles-Simpson plan, Stiglitz argues, is based on increasing the tax burden on middle-class Americans rather than on the wealthiest Americans. Further, Stiglitz insists, the plan overemphasizes the importance of reducing the deficit and proposes cuts to revenue and expenditures that would severely compromise the well-being of working Americans and sacrifice long-term economic growth in favor of short-term gains for the wealthy and corporations. The best way

Joseph E. Stiglitz, "Why I Didn't Sign Deficit Letter," Politico, March 28, 2011. http://www.politico.com/news/stories/0311/52027.html. Copyright © 2011 by Politico. All rights reserved. Reproduced by permission.

to ensure the health of the US economy, he concludes, is to focus on creating jobs, containing health care costs, and closing corporate tax loopholes—not on reducing the budget deficit.

As you read, consider the following questions:

1. Why does Stiglitz say the budget deficit proposal of the Bowles-Simpson commission amounts to "a near-suicide pact"?

2. How can what Stiglitz characterizes as the US history of underinvestment in infrastructure such as education and technology lead to deficit reduction, according to the viewpoint?

3. Why does Stiglitz support raising taxes on the wealthy?

I was asked to sign the letter from a bipartisan group of former chairmen and chairwomen of the Council of Economic Advisers that stresses the importance of deficit reduction and urges the use of the Bowles-Simpson deficit commission's recommendations [referring to the recommendations of the National Commission on Fiscal Responsibility and Reform, chaired by Erskire Bowles and Alan K. Simpson] as the basis for compromise.

The letter's signatories believed that their support would show that there was a core to scientific economics that crosses ideological boundaries. While I agree there is a core set of principles to which all card-carrying economists would (or should) subscribe—resources are limited, incentives matter—I did not sign.

I believe the Bowles-Simpson recommendations represent, to too large an extent, a set of unprincipled political compromises that would lead to a weaker America—with slower growth and a more divided society.

In a white paper written for the Roosevelt Institute, I explain the principles that should underlay deficit reduction and what a deficit reduction package consistent with these could look like.

We Must Put America Back to Work

The ballooning of the deficit since the crisis struck has understandably moved deficit reduction to the center of the debate. But the best way to reduce the deficit is to put America back to work.

Overwhelmingly, the deficit increase has been caused by the enormous shortfall between the economy's potential and actual output. Even as growth has resumed, the "output gap"—reflecting in high unemployment—has persisted. The Bowles-Simpson recommendations, if adopted, would constitute a near-suicide pact: Growth would slow, tax revenues would diminish, the improvement in the deficit would be minimal.

What matters for sustainability is the debt to gross domestic product ratio—and that likely could worsen. This is what we have seen in the similarly poorly designed austerity measures of Greece, Latvia and Ireland; and in earlier such measures in Argentina and East Asia. The International Monetary Fund seems to have learned the lesson—but not the Bowles-Simpson commission.

With monetary policy demonstrably ineffective in pulling us out of our malaise, fiscal policy is the only recourse to putting America back to work. Fortunately, we can simultaneously stimulate the economy now and reduce the deficit in the medium term.

Years of underinvestment in the public sector—in infrastructure, education and technology—mean that there are ample high-return opportunities. Tax revenues generated by the higher short- and long-term growth will more than pay the low interest costs, implying significant reductions in deficits. Any firm that could borrow at terms similar to those

"I'm afraid at times like this with overstretched budgets we all have to make sacrifices," cartoon by Fran, www.CartoonStock.com. Copyright © by Fran. Reproduction rights obtainable from www.CartoonStock.com. Reproduced by permission.

available to the U.S., and with such high return projects, would be foolish to pass up the opportunity.

So, too, increased progressivity of the tax system—shifting the burden from low- and middle-income Americans, who have seen their incomes decline, to upper-income Americans, the only group in the country that has prospered for the last decade—would have double benefits. The shift would stimulate the economy in the short run and reduce the growing divide in the country in the long run.

Increasing Taxes on Top Income Earners Will Raise Needed Revenue

With a quarter of all U.S. income going to the upper 1 percent, and America's middle class actually facing lower incomes than a decade ago, there is only one way to raise more taxes: Tax the top.

A corollary of this inequality is that slight increases in the taxes at the top can raise large amounts of revenue. Just making the tax system fairer and more efficient at the top—eliminating the massive corporate welfare hidden in the tax system and the peculiar provisions that allow the speculators and bankers who helped cause the crisis pay far lower taxes than those who work for their income—would go a long way toward deficit reduction.

The Bowles-Simpson commission is correct in pointing to the middle-class tax expenditures, which encourage excessive spending on health care and housing. But eliminating these provisions should not be considered part of a deficit reduction package. If they were eliminated, the hard-pressed middle class should be protected by corresponding reductions in tax rates.

Moreover, the commission seems insensitive to the consequences of even making commitments today to reduce mortgage deductions in the future—no matter how gradually phased in. Housing prices would fall further; more Americans would see their homes go underwater; there would be more foreclosures, and the ever-suffering middle class would face even more suffering.

Soaring Health Care Costs Must Be Contained

The Bowles-Simpson commission is correct in one conclusion: At the core of the country's long run deficit and debt problem are soaring health care costs. The commission recognized that it had not adequately dealt with this crucial issue. If U.S. health care costs were comparable to those of European countries, which provide better health care to more citizens at lower costs, our long-term deficit would be under control.

But the commission did not point out the implications of attempting to curb costs of the public system for the aged and poor, without reforming that for the rest of the economy. Inevitably, it would mean that the poor and aged would face rationing. They could not compete for the health care services.

In short, redesigning tax and expenditure programs could promote faster economic growth in both the short run and long; increase equity and opportunity, and lower the national debt, and the debt/GDP [gross domestic product] ratio even more.

In my report, I outline the low-hanging fruit that could easily exceed the $4 trillion dollar target set by the Bowles-Simpson commission. For example: (a) The Cold War ended more than two decades ago, but we continue to spend tens of billions on weapons that don't work against enemies that don't exist. Fruitless wars have not increased our security and our military's credibility. Rather, they have undermined both.

We could have more security with less spending. The commission recognized this—but didn't go far enough. Congress and the [President Barack] Obama administration have not gone far enough either.

(b) The health care reform bill did little to eliminate the trillion-dollar giveaway to the drug companies, resulting from restrictions on the ability of government (the largest buyer of drugs) to negotiate prices, in contrast to every other government in the world. While much more can, and should, be done to control health care costs, this little change would make a big difference.

The United States Should Eliminate Tax Breaks to Oil and Mining Companies

Eliminating corporate welfare, both that hidden in our tax systems and in the hidden giveaways of our country's natural resources to oil and gas and mining companies; eliminating the unjustifiable and harmful tax breaks for speculators and companies that keep their money out of the country; and taxing activities that generate large negative externalities— whether the environmental pollution that threatens our health and our children's future, or the financial transactions that brought our country and the world to the brink of ruin—could all easily generate trillions of dollars in revenues. At the same time, they could also create a fairer society, a cleaner environment, and a more stable economy.

Deficit reduction is important. But it is a means to an end—not an end in itself. We need to think about what kind of economy, and what kind of society, we want to create; and how tax and expenditure programs can help achieve those goals.

Bowles-Simpson confuses means with ends and would take us off in directions which would likely be counterproductive. Fortunately, there are alternatives that could do more for deficit reduction, more for putting America back to work now, and more for creating the kind of economy and society we should be striving for in the future.

| *"It is all but impossible to balance the budget when the unemployment rate is above 8.0%."*

Job Growth Will Lead to US Economic Recovery and Deficit Reduction

Dean Baker

Dean Baker is codirector of the Center for Economic and Policy Research based in Washington, DC. In the following viewpoint, he says that recent history shows the last time the United States balanced the budget it was because job growth exceeded expectations. During the 1990s, he explains, there was a federal budget surplus, despite the fact that government policies added billions of dollars to the deficit. This was possible, he insists, because the national unemployment rate was below 5 percent. If the United States could again lower unemployment to this level, Baker concludes, the budget deficit could become a surplus once again. The best way to achieve this is growing the economy with further federal stimulus spending, lowering long-term interest rates, and manipulating monetary policy.

Dean Baker, "The Only Real Solution for Budget Deficits: Growth," *The Guardian*, May 11, 2011. http://www.guardian.co.uk/commentisfree/cifamerica/2011/may/10/economy -public-finance. Copyright © 2011 by the Guardian. All rights reserved. Reproduced by permission.

As you read, consider the following questions:

1. Who does Baker say is the hero in the Democratic version of the story of the budget surplus of the 1990s?

2. What did the CBO predict would be the percentage of growth by 2007, according to the viewpoint?

3. What would be the interest savings if the Federal Reserve bought and held $3 trillion in government bonds, according to Baker?

People in Washington have incredibly bad memories. The last time that the United States balanced its budget was just a decade ago. Even though this is not distant history, almost no one in a policy making position or in the media seems able to remember how the United States managed to go from large deficits at the start of the decade to large surpluses at the end of the decade.

There are two often-told tales about the budget surpluses of the late 1990s: a Democratic story and a Republican story. President [Bill] Clinton is the hero of the Democratic story. In this account, his decision to raise taxes in 1993, along with restraint on spending, was the key to balancing the budget.

The hero in the Republican story is Newt Gingrich. In this story, the Republican Congress that took power in 1995 demanded serious spending constraints. These constraints were ultimately the main factor in balancing the budget.

The Real Cause of Budget Surpluses Is Low Unemployment

Fortunately, we can go behind this "he said/she said" to find the real cause of the switch from large budget deficits to large surpluses. This one is actually easy.

In the spring of 1996, the nonpartisan Congressional Budget Office (CBO), whose numbers are taken as being authoritative in Washington, projected that the government would

Characteristics of Genuine Deficit Hawks

Deficit hawks come in a variety of breeds. There are those who believe that the long-term deficits pose serious risks, but that short-term deficits are necessary and wise during a recession. There are those who believe that deficits are always risky and should be avoided at all costs. Both kinds of hawks are genuine in their concern over our nation's finances and are sincerely committed to working toward a more sustainable federal budget.

Michael Linden,
"How to Spot a Deficit Peacock,"
Center for American Progress, January 20, 2010.
www.americanprogress.org.

have a deficit of $244bn [billion] in 2000, or 2.7% of GDP [gross domestic product]. Instead, the government actually ran a budget surplus in 2000 of almost the same size. This amounted to a shift from deficit to surplus of more than 5.0 percentage points of GDP; an amount that is equal to $750bn given the current size of the economy.

The reason for picking the spring of 1996 as the starting point is that this is after President Clinton's tax increases and spending restraints were all in place. It was also after all the spending restrictions put in place by the Gingrich Congress had already been passed into law. In other words, the CBO knew about all of the deficit reduction measures touted by *both* political parties and it still projected a $244bn budget deficit for 2000. Furthermore, the changes to the budget in the subsequent years went the wrong way. According to CBO's assessment, the legislated changes between 1996 and 2000 actually added $10bn to the budget deficit.

The trick that got us from the large deficit projected for 2000 to the surplus that we actually experienced in that year was, in fact, much stronger than projected growth. CBO projected that growth would average just 2.1%. It actually averaged almost 4.3%. Instead of ending the period with an unemployment rate of 6.0%, unemployment averaged just 4.0% in 2000.

History Teaches Us to Emphasize Growth

It would be helpful if policy makers paid more attention to this history, since it should remind them that even if their primary concern is the deficit, and not economic growth and low unemployment, economic growth may still be the best way to reach their deficit targets. It is all but impossible to balance the budget when the unemployment rate is above 8.0%. By contrast, if we got the unemployment rate back down below 5.0% (where it was before the onset of the recession), we would get most of the way back to a balanced budget—even with no additional changes to the budget.

If the deficit hawk crew could remember back to the 90s, then they might be pushing more aggressively for measures to spur growth. This would include not only fiscal stimulus, but also more expansionary measures from the Federal Reserve [the Fed] board. The Fed has consistently been restrained in its measures to boost the economy because of the whining of the inflation hawks.

The budget hawks should realise that if they really care about deficits, the inflation hawks are their enemies. They should be pushing for more expansionary monetary policy— steps like targeting long-term interest rates or even a somewhat higher inflation rate. There is no reason that the Fed should not be pursuing this path, at least until there is some evidence of inflation posing a problem.

Federal Monetary Policy Should Focus on Raising Exports and Holding Bonds

The Fed, together with the Treasury, could also be pushing for a lower dollar. A monetary policy that is explicitly designed to reduce the value of the dollar would provide a boost to net exports and thereby to economic growth.

Finally, if the Fed opted to hold the bonds that it has purchased through its various quantitative easing programmes, it could directly reduce the deficit. The reasoning here is that the interest paid on these bonds is paid to the Fed and then refunded to the Treasury. It therefore leads to *no net interest burden* to the government. If the Fed bought and held $3tn [trillion] in government bonds, it would lead to interest savings of close to $1.8tn over the course of the next decade.

If the deficit hawks had better memories and a bit of creativity, they would be talking about items like faster growth and increasing the Fed's holdings of government bonds. Unfortunately, our policy makers don't do very well in either the memory or the creativity department. As a result, we are instead discussing the privatisation of Medicare, the block-granting of Medicaid and cutting Social Security. That's Washington for you.

| "It is my belief that a dollar of deficit spending does more damage to job creation than a dollar of taxes."

Deficit Reduction Must Take Place Before Job Growth Can Occur

Peter D. Schiff

Peter D. Schiff is president of Euro Pacific Capital and author of How an Economy Grows and Why It Crashes. *In the following viewpoint, he argues that to create conditions that will grow the economy, the government should balance the budget through major cuts in spending. Schiff asserts that the kinds of jobs that are created by increased government spending on infrastructure programs are only a temporary fix. Also temporary, Schiff says, are the effects of offering tax credits for employers for hiring veterans and the unemployed. Schiff concludes that government regulations and spending discourage job growth, and that both must be severely curtailed in order for economic growth to occur.*

As you read, consider the following questions:

1. How could federal government spending on infrastructure improve an economy in the long run, according to Schiff?

Peter Schiff, "How the Government Can Create Jobs," Testimony Offered to the House Subcommittee on Regulatory Affairs, Stimulus Oversight and Government Spending, pp. 1–6. September 13, 2011.

2. What does Schiff say that a $4,000 credit for hiring the unemployed will likely cause?

3. How, according to Schiff, would discontinuing long-term unemployment benefits lead to job growth?

Despite the understandable human tendency to help others, government spending cannot be a net creator of jobs. Indeed many efforts currently under consideration by the administration and Congress will actively destroy jobs. These initiatives must stop. While it is easy to see how a deficit-financed government program can lead to the creation of a specific job, it is much harder to see how other jobs are destroyed by the diversion of capital and resources. It is also difficult to see how the bigger budget deficits sap the economy of vitality, destroying jobs in the process.

In a free market, jobs are created by profit-seeking businesses with access to capital. Unfortunately, government taxes and regulation diminish profits, and deficit spending and artificially low interest rates inhibit capital formation. As a result, unemployment remains high, and will likely continue to rise until policies are reversed.

It is my belief that a dollar of deficit spending does more damage to job creation than a dollar of taxes. That is because taxes (particularly those targeting the middle or lower income groups) have their greatest impact on spending, while deficits more directly impact savings and investment. Contrary to the beliefs held by many professional economists, spending does not make an economy grow. Savings and investment are far more determinative. Any program that diverts capital into consumption and away from savings and investment will diminish future economic growth and job creation.

Not All Jobs Are Equal

Creating jobs is easy for government, but all jobs are not equal. Paying people to dig ditches and fill them up does society no good. On balance these "jobs" diminish the economy by wasting scarce land, labor and capital. We do not want jobs for the sake of work, but for the goods and services they produce. As it has a printing press, the government could mandate employment for all, as did the Soviet Union. But if these jobs are not productive, and government jobs rarely are, society is no better for it.

This is also true of the much vaunted "infrastructure spending." Any funds directed toward infrastructure deprive the economy of resources that might otherwise have funded projects that the market determines have greater economic value. Infrastructure can improve an economy in the long run, but only if the investments succeed in raising productivity more than the cost of the project itself. In the interim, infrastructure costs are burdens that an economy must bear, not a means in themselves.

Unfortunately, our economy is so weak and indebted that we simply cannot currently afford many of these projects. The labor and other resources that would be diverted to finance them are badly needed elsewhere.

Although it was labeled and hyped as a "jobs plan," the new $447 billion initiative announced last night [September 12, 2011] by President [Barack] Obama is merely another government stimulus program in disguise. Like all previous stimuli that have been injected into the economy over the past three years, this round of borrowing and spending will act as an economic sedative rather than a stimulant. I am convinced that a year from now there will be even more unemployed Americans than there are today, likely resulting in additional deficit-financed stimulus that will again make the situation worse.

The president asserted that the spending in the plan will be "paid for" and will not add to the deficit. Conveniently, he offered no details about how this will be achieved. Most likely he will make nonbinding suggestions that future Congresses "pay" for this spending by cutting budgets five to ten years in the future. In the meantime, money to fund the stimulus has to come from someplace. Either the government will borrow it legitimately from private sources, or the Federal Reserve will print. Either way, the adverse consequences will damage economic growth and job creation, and lower the living standards of Americans.

There can be no doubt that some jobs will in fact be created by this plan. However, it is much more difficult to identify the jobs that it destroys or prevents from coming into existence. Here's a case in point: the $4,000 tax credit for hiring new workers who have been unemployed for six months or more. The subsidy may make little difference in effecting the high end of the job market, but it really could make an impact on minimum wage jobs where rather than expanding employment it will merely increase turnover.

Since an employer need only hire a worker for 6 months to get the credit, for a full-time employee, the credit effectively reduces the $7.25 minimum wage (from the employer's perspective) to only $3.40 per hour for a six-month hire. While minimum wage jobs would certainly offer no enticement to those collecting unemployment benefits, the lower effective rate may create some opportunities for teenagers and some low-skilled individuals whose unemployment benefits have expired. However, most of these jobs will end after six months so employers can replace those workers with others to get an additional tax credit.

Tax Credits Encourage Abuse of the System

Of course the numbers get even more compelling for employers to provide returning veterans with temporary minimum wage jobs, as the higher $5,600 tax credit effectively reduces the minimum wage to only $1.87 per hour. If an employer hires a "wounded warrior," the tax credit is $9,600 that effectively reduces the six-month minimum wage by $9.23 to negative $1.98 per hour. This will encourage employers to hire a "wounded warrior" even if there is nothing for the employee to do. Such an incentive may encourage such individuals to acquire multiple no-show jobs from numerous employers. As absurd as this sounds, history has shown that when government creates incentives, the public will twist themselves into pretzels to qualify for the benefit.

The plan creates incentives for employers to replace current minimum wage workers with new workers just to get the tax credit. Low skill workers are the easiest to replace as training costs are minimal. The laid off workers can collect unemployment for six months and then be hired back in a manner that allows the employer to claim the credit. The only problem is that the former worker may prefer collecting extended unemployment benefits to working for the minimum wage!

The $4,000 credit for hiring the unemployed as well as the explicit penalties for discriminating against the long-term unemployed will result in a situation where employers will be far more likely to interview and hire applicants who have been unemployed for just under six months. Under the law, employers would be wise to refuse to interview anyone who has been unemployed for more than six months, as any subsequent decision not to hire could be met with a lawsuit. However, to get the tax credit, they would be incentivized to interview applicants who have been unemployed for just under six months. If they are never hired, there can be no risk of a lawsuit, but if they are hired, the start date can be planned to qualify for the credit.

The result will simply create classes of winners (those unemployed for four or five months) and losers (the newly unemployed and the long-term unemployed). Ironically, the law banning discrimination against long-term unemployed will make it much harder for such individuals to find jobs.

At present, I am beginning to feel that overregulation of business and employment, and an overly complex and punitive tax code, is currently a bigger impediment to job growth than is our horrific fiscal and monetary policies. As a business owner, I know that reckless government policy can cause no end of unintended consequences.

Regulations Impede Job Growth

As I see it, here are the biggest obstacles preventing job growth:

1. *Monetary Policy*

Interest rates are much too low. Cheap money produced both the stock market and real estate bubbles, and is currently facilitating a bubble in government debt. When this bubble bursts, the repercussions will dwarf the shock produced by the financial crisis of 2008. Interest rates must be raised to bring on a badly needed restructuring of our economy. No doubt an environment of higher rates will cause short-term pain. But we need to move from a "borrow and spend" economy to a "save and produce" economy. This cannot be done with ultra-low interest rates. In the short-term GNP [gross national product] will need to contract. There will be a pickup in transitory unemployment. Real estate and stock prices will fall. Many banks will fail. There will be more foreclosures. Government spending will have to be slashed. Entitlements will have to be cut. Many voters will be angry. But such an environment will lay the foundation upon which a real recovery can be built.

The government must allow our bubble economy to fully deflate. Asset prices, wages, and spending must fall; interest rates, production, and savings must rise. Resources, including labor, must be reallocated away from certain sectors, such as government, services, finance, health care, and educations, and be allowed into manufacturing, mining, oil and gas, agriculture, and other goods-producing fields. We will never borrow and spend our way out of a crisis caused by too much borrowing and spending. The only way out is to reverse course.

2. *Fiscal Policy*

To create conditions that foster growth, the government should balance the budget with major cuts in government spending and severely reform and simplify the tax code. It would be preferable if all corporate and personal taxes could be replaced by a national sales tax. Our current tax system discourages the activities that we need most: hard work, production, savings, investment, and risk taking. Instead, it incentivizes consumption and debt. We should tax people when they spend their wealth, not when they create it. High marginal income tax rates inflict major damage to job creation, as the tax is generally paid out of money that otherwise would have been used to finance capital investment and job creation.

3. *Regulation*

Regulations have substantially increased the costs and risks associated with job creation. Employers are subjected to all sorts of onerous regulations, taxes, and legal liability. The act of becoming an employer should be made as easy as possible. Instead we have made it more difficult. In fact, among small business owners, limiting the number of employees is generally a goal. This is not a consequence of the market, but of a rational desire on the part of business owners to limit their cost and legal liabilities. They would prefer to hire workers, but these added burdens make it preferable to seek out alternatives.

In my own business, securities regulations have prohibited me from hiring brokers for more than three years. I was even fined fifteen thousand dollars expressly for hiring too many brokers in 2008. In the process, I incurred more than $500,000 in legal bills to mitigate a more severe regulatory outcome as a result of hiring too many workers. I have also been prohibited from opening up additional offices. I had a major expansion plan that would have resulted in my creating hundreds of additional jobs. Regulations have forced me to put those jobs on hold.

Government Spending Interferes with Economic Growth

Absent a significant rise in revenue beyond the historical level of GDP [gross domestic product], spending on Social Security, Medicare, and interest on the debt could squeeze out all other areas of the budget. Taxes could, in principle, be increased to cover these costs, but the unprecedented tax levels required would have an extremely negative impact on employment, wage growth, and our ability to compete internationally. . . .

Even if Congress and the president adopted huge tax increases—as much as $3 trillion over the next 10 years—government spending would still outpace this huge revenue increase. The result will be increasing government borrowing and debt. The accumulating debt will increasingly crowd out more productive private sector investment, and thereby squeeze capital formation.

That in turn will lead to productivity declines and lower rates of real economic growth, materially affecting living standards. . . .

In short, the debt arising from government spending trends is sacrificing the prosperity of future generations.

Paul Ryan, "Introduction,"
A Roadmap for America's Future, January 27, 2010.
www.roadmap.republicans.budget.house.gov.

In addition, the added cost of security regulations have forced me to create an offshore brokerage firm to handle foreign accounts that are now too expensive to handle from the United States. Revenue and jobs that would have been created in the U.S. are now being created abroad instead. In addition, I am moving several asset management jobs from Newport Beach, California, to Singapore.

As Congress turns up the heat, more of my capital will continue to be diverted to my foreign companies, creating jobs and tax revenues abroad rather than in the United States.

Removing Regulations and Benefits Will Spur Real Job Growth

To encourage real and lasting job growth, the best thing the government can do is to make it as easy as possible for business to hire and employ people. This means cutting down on workplace regulations. It also means eliminating the punitive aspects of employment law that cause employers to think twice about hiring. To be blunt, the easier employees are to fire, the higher the likelihood they will be hired. Some steps Congress could take now include [the following].

a. Abolish the Federal Minimum Wage. Minimum wages have never raised the wages of anyone and simply draw an arbitrary line that separates the employable from the unemployable. Just like prices, wages are determined by supply and demand. The demand for workers is a function of how much productivity a worker can produce. Setting the wage at $7.25 simply means that only those workers who can produce goods and services that create more than $7.25 (plus all additional payroll associated costs) per hour are eligible for jobs. Those who can't, become permanently unemployable. The artificial limits encourage employers to look to minimize hires and to automate wherever possible.

By putting many low-skill workers (such as teenagers) below the line, the minimum wage prevents crucial on-the-job training, which could provide workers with the experience and skills needed to earn higher wages.

b. Repeal All Federal Workplace Anti-Discrimination Laws. One of the reasons unemployment is so high among minorities is that business owners (particularly small business) are wary of legal liability associated with various categories of protected minorities. The fear of litigation, and the costly judgments that can ensue, are real. Given that it is nearly impossible for an employer to control all the aspects of the workplace environment, litigation risk is a tangible consideration. Given all the legal avenues afforded by legislation, minority employees are much more likely to sue employers. To avoid this, some employers simply look to avoid this outcome by sticking with less risky employee categories. It is not racism that causes this discrimination, but a rational desire to mitigate liability. The reality is that a true free market would punish employers that discriminate based on race or other criteria irrelevant to job performance. That is because businesses that hire based strictly on merit would have a competitive advantage. Antidiscrimination laws tilted the advantage to those who discriminate.

c. Repeal All Laws Mandating Employment Terms Such as Workplace Conditions, Overtime, Benefits, Leave, Medical Benefits, Etc. Employment is a voluntary relationship between two parties. The more room the parties have to negotiate and agree on their own terms, the more likely a job will be created. Rules imposed from the top create inefficiencies that limit employment opportunities. Employee benefits are a cost of employment, and high-value employees have all the bargaining power they need to extract benefits from employers. They are free to search for the best benefits they can get just as they search for the best wages.

Companies that do not offer benefits will lose employees to companies that do. Just as employees are free to leave companies at will, so too should employers be free to terminate an employee without fear of costly repercussions. Individuals should not gain rights because they are employees, and individuals should not lose rights because they become employers.

d. Abolish Extended Unemployment Benefits. In addition to being a source of emergency funds, unemployment benefits over time become more of a disincentive to employment than anything else (although the disincentive diminishes with the worker's skill level—i.e., high-wage workers are unlikely to forego a high-wage job opportunity to preserve unemployment benefits). For marginally skilled workers, unemployment insurance is a major factor in determining if a job should be taken or not.

Even if unemployment pays a significant fraction of the wage a worker would get with a full-time job, the money may be enough to convince the worker to stay home. After all, there are costs associated with having a job. Not only does a worker pay payroll and income taxes on any wages he earns, the loss of unemployment benefits itself acts as a tax. Plus workers must pay for such job-related expenses as transportation, clothing, restaurant meals, dry cleaning, and child care, and they must forgo other work that they could do in their free time (providing care for loved ones, home improvement, etc.).

Understandably, most people also find leisure time preferable to work. As a result, any job that does not offer a major monetary advantage to unemployment benefits will likely be turned down. This entrenches unemployment insurance recipients into a class of permanently unemployed workers.

It is no accident that employment increases immediately after unemployment insurance expires for many categories of workers. In fact, many individuals will seek to max out their benefits and remain unemployed until those benefits expire. If they work at all, it will be for cash under the table, so as not to leave any money on the table.

| "The drumbeat of deficit hysterics thumping in self-righteous panic grows louder by the day."

Debate over Deficit Reduction Is More About Politics than the Economy

Christopher Hayes

Christopher Hayes is editor at large of the Nation *and host of* Up with Chris Hayes *on MSNBC. In the following viewpoint, he argues that the hysteria being generated by politicians over the deficit is unwarranted and detracts from discussions of important issues such as unemployment. He draws a comparison between the deficit debate and the debate that preceded the 2003 start of the US-led war in Iraq. At that time, he maintains, a vocal majority of Republicans demanded action despite a lack of clear evidence to support their claims and were largely unopposed by Democrats; this, he argues, is also the case with the debate over the deficit. Hayes blames the deficit on excessive spending on the wars in Iraq and Afghanistan, tax cuts during the President George W. Bush administration, and the economic recession. The current debate over the deficit, he concludes, obscures the origins of the deficit.*

Christopher Hayes, "Deficits of Mass Destruction," *The Nation*, August 2, 2010. Copyright © 2010 by The Nation. All rights reserved. Reproduced by permission.

As you read, consider the following questions:

1. What does Hayes say that conservatives and neoliberals care about?

2. Why, according to Hayes, are advisors to the president reluctant to spend more to create jobs?

3. According to the author, what percentage of Americans support additional government spending to create jobs and stimulate the economy?

If you've been paying attention this past decade, it won't surprise you to learn that the country's policy elites are in the midst of a destructive, well-nigh unhinged discussion about the future of the nation. But even by the degraded standards of the Washington establishment, the growing panic over government debt is shocking.

First, the facts. Nearly the entire deficit for this year [2010] and those projected into the near and medium terms are the result of three things: the ongoing wars in Afghanistan and Iraq, the [President George W.] Bush tax cuts and the recession. The solution to our fiscal situation is: end the wars, allow the tax cuts to expire and restore robust growth. Our long-term structural deficits will require us to control health care inflation the way countries with single-payer systems do.

But right now we face a joblessness crisis that threatens to pitch us into a long, ugly period of low growth, the kind of lost decade that will cause tremendous misery, degrade the nation's human capital, undermine an entire cohort of young workers for years and blow a hole in the government's bank sheet. The best chance we have to stave off this scenario is more government spending to nurse the economy back to health. The economy may be alive, but that doesn't mean it's healthy. There's a reason you keep taking antibiotics even after you start to feel better.

Hysteria over the Deficit Is Growing

And yet: The drumbeat of deficit hysterics thumping in self-righteous panic grows louder by the day. Judging by its schedule and online video, this year's Aspen Ideas Festival was an open-air orgy of anti-deficit moaning. The festival is a good window into elite preoccupations, and that its opening forum featured ominous warnings of future bankruptcy from Niall Ferguson, Mort Zuckerman and David Gergen does not bode well. Nor does the fact that there was a panel called "America's Looming Fiscal Emergency: How to Balance the Books." This attitude isn't confined to pundits. The heads of [President Barack] Obama's fiscal commission have called projected deficits a "cancer."

The hysteria has reached such a pitch that Republican senators (joined by Nebraska Democrat Ben Nelson) have filibustered an extension of unemployment benefits because it was not offset by spending cuts. Keep in mind, the cost of the extension for people unlucky enough to be caught in the jaws of the worst recession in thirty years is $35 billion. The bill would increase the debt by less than 0.3 percent.

This all seems eerily familiar. The conversation—if it can be called that—about deficits recalls the national conversation about war in the run-up to the [March 2003] invasion of Iraq. From one day to the next, what was once accepted by the establishment as tolerable—Saddam Hussein—became intolerable, a crisis of such pressing urgency that "serious people" were required to present their ideas about how to deal with it. Once the burden of proof shifted from those who favored war to those who opposed it, the argument was lost.

Two Manufactured Crises

We are poised on the same tipping point with regard to the debt. Amid official unemployment of 9.5 percent and a global contraction, we shouldn't even be talking about deficits in the short run. Yet these days, entrance into the club of the "seri-

Responsibility for Damaging Deficit-Based Policy Is Shared

The policy disaster of the past two years wasn't just the result of G.O.P. [Republican] obstructionism, which wouldn't have been so effective if the policy elite . . . hadn't agreed that deficit reduction, not job creation, should be our main priority.

Paul Krugman, "The Wrong Worries,"
New York Times, August 4, 2011.

ous" requires not a plan for reducing unemployment but a plan to do battle with the invisible and as yet unmaterialized international bond traders preparing an attack on the dollar.

Perhaps the most egregious aspect of the selling of the Iraq War was its false pretext. It never really was about weapons of mass destruction [WMDs], as Paul Wolfowitz [former US deputy secretary of defense] admitted. WMDs were just "what everyone could agree on." So it is with deficits. Conservatives and their neoliberal allies don't really care about deficits; they care about austerity—about gutting the welfare state and redistributing wealth upward. That's the objective. Deficits are just what they can all agree on, the WMDs of this manufactured crisis. Senator Jon Kyl of Arizona, speaking on FOX, has come out and admitted as much. All new spending increases must be offset, he said, but "you should never have to offset the cost of a deliberate decision to reduce tax rates on Americans." So there you have it.

Remember that the Iraq War might have been prevented had more congressional Democrats stood up to oppose it. Instead, many of those who privately knew the entire enterprise was a colossal disaster in the making buckled to right-wing pressure and pundit hawks and voted for it. That mistake is being repeated. Despite White House economists' full realization of the need for stimulus in the face of astronomically high unemployment, the *New York Times* has reported that the political minds inside the White House, David Axelrod and Rahm Emanuel, have decided that the public has no appetite for increased spending. "It's my job to report what the public mood is," Axelrod explained. He then showed up on ABC's *This Week* to wave the white flag, saying that the president would continue to press to extend unemployment benefits; conspicuously omitted was any mention of aid to state governments, which had originally been included in the president's June letter to Congress asking for a new stimulus package.

Public Opinion Favors Spending and Entitlements

There is hope, however: The public is nowhere near as obsessed with the deficit as are those in Washington. According to a *USA Today*/Gallup poll, 60 percent of Americans support "additional government spending to create jobs and stimulate the economy," with 38 percent opposed. A Hart Research Associates poll published in June showed that two-thirds of Americans favor continuing unemployment benefits. There is also very little public appetite for "entitlement reform," [also known as] cutting Social Security.

The lesson of the Iraq War is that over the long haul, good politics and good policy can't be separated. If the White House is tempted to support bad policy in the short term because it seems less risky politically, it should give [2004 Democratic presidential candidate Senator] John Kerry a call and ask him how that worked out for him with Iraq.

> *"It is not the size of the deficit/public debt in either absolute or relative terms that matters, but rather its actual or prospective economic effects."*

Poor Economic Policy Does More Harm to the Economy than a Large Deficit

Daniel Berger

Daniel Berger is an attorney, author, journalist, and political commentator who specializes in the US economy. In the following viewpoint, he argues that concerns over the economic impact of the deficit are wrongheaded because they fail to take into consideration the fact that deficit increases are temporary effects of economic downturns. When the economy improves, Berger contends, the deficit will be lower. He asserts that Republican-backed policies that cut taxes and federal spending were responsible for part of the financial crisis that has made it more difficult for the United States to recover from the economic downturn.

As you read, consider the following questions:

1. What three factors does Berger say are involved in possible adverse effects of the deficit/national debt?

Daniel Berger, "The Deficit: Size Doesn't Matter," *Next New Deal*, blog of the Roosevelt Institute, November 18, 2009. http://www.nextnewdeal.net/deficit-size-doesnt-matter. Copyright © 2009 the Roosevelt Institute. All rights reserved. Reproduced by permission.

2. To what are at least half of the record 2009–2010 deficits attributable, according to Berger?

3. Why did the Republican Party intentionally advocate full employment deficits, according to the viewpoint?

Criticism of extensive efforts of the national government to address—and overcome—the current economic emergency has taken on essentially three forms: on philosophical grounds (that the stimulus and the bank bailout represent unwarranted compromises of the free enterprise system), on policy grounds (that they will result in dangerous budget deficits and increases of public debt) and political grounds (that they are sellouts to the banks and special interests). Of the three critiques, the one relating to fiscal policy is generally regarded by conventional wisdom as the most serious. The argument is that increased budget deficits and national debt are unsustainable and will harm the national economy more than they will help. This position is, at best, factually wrong and exaggerated. At worst, it fails to take into account the elementary distinction between the short-run cyclical and the long-term structural condition of the economy.

The federal budget deficit for 2009 and 2010 is estimated to be between $1.5–2 trillion or in excess of 10% of GPD [gross domestic product]. This exceeds the existing peacetime record of 6% set in 1983. The corresponding figures relating to the national debt reflect that in the 1990s, the ratio of national debt to GDP peaked at 50%, then fell to 33% in 2001, its lowest level for the preceding 20 years. It is estimated to go to 60% in 2010, its highest level since 1950.

While most critics of federal spending to contain the financial and economic crises seem to decry any spending which increases the deficit, it must be acknowledged that estimated levels of both the deficit and national debt are large in historic terms. *However, it is not the size of the deficit/public debt in either absolute or relative terms that matters, but rather its actual or prospective economic effects.*

The Size and Impact of the Deficit Are Overstated

To begin with, the size of the deficit (and projections for the debt) attributable to the economic recovery program are overstated for the period after 2010 and fail to take into account their short-run cyclical behavior and the impact of renewed growth in 2010 and thereafter. The deficit consists of both increases in spending addressing the economic crisis and declines in tax revenue caused by the downturn. Both this type of spending and tax revenue declines are temporary. Once self-sustaining growth resumes, these two variables reverse. Thus, renewed growth will naturally result in dramatically lower deficits (all things being equal).

Whatever the net numbers after 2010, possible adverse effects of the deficit/national debt basically involve impacts on interest rates, the dollar and inflation. The possible effects on interest rates could be both short run and long term. It has been said that the deficit might raise bond yields now before a self-sustaining recovery sets in, thereby choking it off. In the longer run, it is argued that interest rates might go up because a persistent deficit would cause inflation or because of "crowding out" of private investment as available funds are soaked up by financing of the public debt.

Neither prospect seems particularly likely or evident in the next 5 years. As to the short run, the suggestion is that the market for U.S. Treasury obligations will be inundated by new financings and will require much higher interest rates for Treasury obligations to sell. But current weak economic activity is dominating the Treasury market, and interest rates are at rock-bottom levels. As the last interest rate cycle demonstrated, this situation can persist indefinitely until the Fed

[Federal Reserve, the U.S. central banking system] decides to lift short-term interest rates.

As to higher inflation, to be sure, the Fed has taken extraordinary steps to supply liquidity [ability to buy and sell] to the financial system, including engaging in a type of quantitative easing [monetary policy employed when central banks purchase assets for a particular amount of money]. The argument appears to be that these actions have resulted in an extraordinary expansion of the money supply, which is necessarily inflationary. We should be so lucky. For the foreseeable future, deflation—not inflation—is the problem. Generally, expansion of the money supply—even a radical expansion—will only produce inflation when the economy is at full employment.

It has also been argued that the deficit and/or sovereign indebtedness of the U.S. will inevitably cause a dollar collapse and foreign capital flight, thereby also raising interest rate and choking off growth. However, there is little evidence, thus far, for these effects. Indeed, the global financial and economic crises have affected other currencies more adversely than the dollar. The dollar collapse argument really amounts to the proposition that the U.S.'s already heavy reliance on external financing cannot absorb additional substantial burdens. Although a complex subject, the external financing requirements (previously to finance the U.S.'s current account deficit) are in flux, as the U.S. is in the process of rebuilding its national savings rate and curbing its imports. Heightened national savings also suggest that financing of public debt will not crowd out private investment, either.

Spending and Financing Have Averted Economic Collapse

As the above demonstrates, there is currently no credible case that steps of the national government to meet the national economic emergency, by themselves, will cause more harm than good, let alone will cause the much ballyhooed economic calamity forecast by critics of the economic stimulus and the bank bailout. Indeed, far from representing fiscal irresponsibility, they are designed to—and have been effective in—staving off economic calamity.

This is not to say that deficits and public debt loads could never adversely affect the U.S. economy in the foreseeable future. At most, and, indeed, only in conjunction with other unpaid-for federal spending could the cumulative effect of spending to save the economy constitute a problem. Moreover, there is no redline danger point beyond which deficits or national debt create a so-called deficit/debt "wall" which will stop the economy in its tracks. Most serious studies show that we are a long way from that point.

There is, however, one aspect of the deficit/public debt problem which must be considered. The [President Barack] Obama administration has not been budgeting and spending on a clean slate. Rather, it inherited a large structural deficit from the prior administration. Indeed, at least half of the record 2009–10 deficits are attributable to [President George W.] Bush's cynical and reckless economic policies which involved running large deficits during periods of prosperity. These deficits of choice involved two wholly avoidable policy fiascos: The Bush tax cuts and the Iraq War—Bush's two signature policy initiatives which were never paid for.

Fiscally Irresponsible Tax Cuts Contributed to the Financial Crisis

In addition to contributing half of the deficit and debt increase at their peaks, the tax cuts and increased spending of the Bush years when the economy was at full employment represent fiscal irresponsibility in the extreme. Imagine where we would be now if the substantial surplus projected for 2009–2010 when President Bill Clinton left office had been available to handle the economic emergency.

The Republican Party intentionally advocated full employment deficits for political reasons, i.e., to force a wholesale abandonment of federal spending except for national defense—the single most wasteful spending item in the budget—by creating an artificial fiscal emergency which would impose forced spending reductions. Unfortunately, the Republicans did not anticipate the financial crisis and the ensuing economic emergency that their reckless economic policies were directly responsible in causing. By creating the artificial emergency, the Bush budget deficits—and the frittering away of the surplus—have undermined the political will of the nation to stave off and exit from the economic downturn and to do what is necessary to ensure the resumption of acceptable rates of non-inflationary long-term growth—exactly what the Republicans wrongly decry about the federal stimulus and bank bailouts. Such obvious hypocrisy and sophistry does not deserve to be taken seriously from a policy perspective. It should be regarded as pure political posturing which has sacrificed the national interests to efforts to cling to political power.

In addition to factual and policy misconceptions about the likely effects of the deficit and national debt over the next 5 years and the historical amnesia of the deficit hawks, current criticism of government spending and budget deficits essentially ignores or conflates short-run cyclical and long-run secular effects. As noted, the deficit will shrink as a result of renewed self-sustaining economic growth which will necessarily raise tax revenues. Indeed, it is a prerequisite for regaining control over both the deficit and the debt as demonstrated by the Clinton years. At that point, we will be left to contend with the structural deficit created by the Bush tax cuts and bequeathed to the nation by Bush and the Republican-controlled Congress. Oh, remember them? That is why it is absolutely essential that the Bush tax cuts be permitted to expire.

At some point, there needs to be a serious conversation between the responsible part of the political leadership in this country and the public about fiscal responsibility and taxes.

Author's note: This analysis was made in 2009 and assumed a self-sustaining recovery by the end of 2010. In fact, a self-sustaining recovery did not occur until 2012. However, the author stands by the analytical features of the article and its basic conclusions.

Periodical and Internet Sources Bibliography

The following articles have been selected to supplement the diverse views presented in this chapter.

Michael Bowman	"'Do Nothing' Option for US Deficit Reduction Explored," *Voice of America*, November 23, 2011. www.voanews.com.
John Carney	"Do Republicans Care About Budget Deficits?," *CNBC.com*, December 13, 2011. www.cnbc.com.
Victor Davis Hanson	"Deficits and Depression," *National Review Online*, October 14, 2010. www.nationalreview.com.
James Ledbetter	"Three Reasons Conservatives Should Oppose a Balanced Budget Amendment," *The Great Debate*, August 1, 2011. http://blogs.reuters.com.
Yuval Levin	"Liberals Playing to Type," *Weekly Standard*, November 21, 2011.
Rick Moran	"Obama's Demagogy on the Deficit," *FrontPageMag.com*, April 14, 2011. http://frontpagemag.com.
Eugene Robinson	"Best Solutions to Federal Deficit Are Progressive," *Arizona Daily Star*, July 9, 2011.
Diane Lim Rogers	"In Budget Battle, Voters Are the 'Adults in the Room,'" *Christian Science Monitor*, December 28, 2011.
Michael Warren	"IMF Cautions About Dangers of Budget Deficit," *Weekly Standard*, June 17, 2011.
David Weinberger	"Do Budget Deficits Reflect American Character?," *The Foundry*, March 8, 2012. http://blog.heritage.org.

OPPOSING
VIEWPOINTS®
SERIES

CHAPTER 2

What Role Should
Taxes Play in
Deficit Reduction?

Chapter Preface

One of the central debates regarding the US deficit is whether taxes should be raised to eliminate some of the gap between what the government takes in and what it spends. In the run-up to the 2012 presidential election, the candidates' stand on taxes highlight the differences in their approach to the deficit.

Republican Mitt Romney has called for an overhaul of the nation's tax code, the rules that people must follow as they file their taxes, which is something that President Barack Obama has also endorsed. But sharp differences between the two candidates become apparent when comparing their plans for tax cuts.

Key to Romney's tax plan is a permanent, across-the-board 20 percent cut in marginal tax rates, the percentage of taxes on extra income. He has proposed a repeal of the alternative minimum tax—the rate paid on income above a set threshold—and the estate tax, which is a tax applied to the transfer of a person's assets at death. For those whose taxable income is less than $200,000, Romney would eliminate taxes on interest, dividends, and capital gains in their investments. Romney's tax plan, analysts have concluded, would result in a significant loss in revenues that would greatly contribute to the nation's deficit.

Obama has proposed raising revenues by closing tax loopholes, which are exemptions and other methods of reducing the amount of taxes owed on income, in the tax code through reforms. He has pointed out that a third of the four hundred highest income earners paid an average of 15 percent in taxes in 2008. He has supported raising taxes on those making more than $250,000. He has also reminded voters that he signed eighteen tax cuts for small businesses and extended the payroll tax cut for all American workers and their families during his presidency that he says put an extra $1,000 in the typical middle-class family's pocket each year.

As part of his 2012 budget plan, Obama would raise taxes for some and lower them for others. In 2015, he has explained, about a third of American households would see their taxes go up, and about one in six would see them drop. Almost all wealthy Americans would end up paying a lot more: 98 percent of those in the top 1 percent of income earners would face tax increases averaging almost $110,000 annually, primarily because Obama would let the tax cuts instituted during President George W. Bush's administration expire for those taxpayers.

As the candidates prepared to square off on the issues, others on the Republican side were taking positions of their own. Representative Paul Ryan put forward a budget that called for an average tax cut of $265,000 for those making $1 million or more. Half of those making between $20,000 and $30,000 would get no tax cut at all.

The role of taxes in deficit reduction is examined in the viewpoints in the following chapter, which includes discussions on whether taxes should be raised, whether they should be raised only for the affluent, and whether tax reform will help lower the deficit.

| *"Relative to the size of the economy, federal revenues are currently at their lowest level in 60 years."*

Raising Taxes Can Help Reduce the Budget Deficit

Congressional Budget Office

The Congressional Budget Office (CBO) is mandated to provide the US Congress with objective, nonpartisan, and timely analyses to aid in economic and budgetary decisions. In the following viewpoint, the CBO reports that in 2010 tax revenues were the lowest in sixty years, and it goes on to detail the effect of the tax revenues on the economy. Tax revenue, the CBO explains, is closely tied to the overall health of the economy, and increasing it could help to offset the deficit and safeguard against future economic downturns. The manner in which tax revenue is increased, the CBO concludes, must take into consideration fairness to taxpayers as well as effects on businesses and the economy in general.

As you read, consider the following questions:

1. What three criteria do economists use to evaluate how a tax policy is working, according to the viewpoint?

Congressional Budget Office, "4: Revenue Options," *Reducing the Deficit: Spending and Revenue Options*, March 2011, pp. 129–136.

2. According to the viewpoint, what are tax expenditures?

3. According to the Congressional Budget Office, what tax rate did households in the top 1 percent of the income distribution face in 2007?

In 2010, the federal government collected roughly $2.2 trillion in revenues. Individual income taxes were the largest source, accounting for nearly 42 percent of total revenues. Social insurance taxes (primarily payroll taxes collected to support Social Security and Medicare) provided another 40 percent. About 9 percent of revenues last year came from corporate income taxes, with other receipts—from excise taxes, estate and gift taxes, earnings of the Federal Reserve System, customs duties, and miscellaneous fees and fines—making up the remaining 10 percent.

Trends in Revenues

Relative to the size of the economy, federal revenues are currently at their lowest level in 60 years. In both 2009 and 2010, revenues equaled 14.9 percent of gross domestic product (GDP). By comparison, they averaged about 18 percent of GDP between 1971 and 2010, peaking at 20.6 percent of GDP in 2000.

The variation in total revenues as a percentage of GDP over time has resulted primarily from ups and downs in individual income tax receipts and, to a lesser extent, from swings in corporate income tax receipts. Revenues from individual income taxes, which have averaged about 8 percent of GDP since 1971, have ranged from a high of 10.2 percent (in 2000) to a low of 6.2 percent (in 2010). The volatility of those revenues stems from two factors. First, a substantial share of the base for individual income taxes is nonwage income (such as capital gains realizations and noncorporate business income), which varies widely over the business cycle. Second, legislative changes often produce significant shifts in individual income taxes. Receipts from corporate income taxes are also quite volatile over the business cycle. They have changed especially dramatically in the past few years—from 2.7 percent of GDP in 2007, the largest share in almost 30 years, to 1.0 percent of GDP in 2009, the smallest share since the 1930s. Because corporate income tax receipts have averaged only 2 percent of GDP over the past 40 years, however, their swings generally have a much smaller impact on total revenues than do the ups and downs in individual income tax receipts.

Social insurance taxes, by contrast, have been a fairly stable source of federal revenues over the years. Receipts from those taxes increased as a percentage of GDP during the 1970s and 1980s as tax rates, the number of people required to pay those taxes, and the share of wages subject to the taxes grew. For the past two decades, however, legislation has not had a substantial effect on social insurance taxes, and the primary base for those taxes—wages and salaries—has varied less as a share of GDP than have other sources of income.

Revenues from other taxes and fees declined relative to the size of the economy over the 1971–2010 period. The main reason is that receipts from excise taxes—which are levied on such goods and services as gasoline, alcohol, tobacco, and air travel—have steadily dwindled as a share of GDP over time, largely because most of those taxes are levied on the quantity rather than the value of goods, and rates have generally not kept up with inflation.

Looking ahead, revenues are projected to grow at a slower pace than GDP this year [2011] and then at a much faster rate. The Congressional Budget Office (CBO) estimates that if current laws remain unchanged, revenues will increase by 3 percent in 2011, to more than $2.2 trillion. As a share of GDP, however, they will fall slightly, to 14.8 percent. Thereafter, revenues are projected to rise rapidly under current law, reaching

19.9 percent of GDP by 2014. About three-quarters of that increase stems from the effects of scheduled changes to the tax code. . . .

The rest of the projected increase in revenues as a percentage of GDP through 2014 is largely attributable to the effects of improvement in the economy. CBO expects that as the economy continues to recover from the recession, wages and salaries, capital gains realizations, and other taxable income will grow more rapidly than GDP.

Under the current law assumptions of CBO's baseline projections, revenues will keep outpacing GDP for the remainder of the 10-year projection period. By 2021, total revenues are projected to rise to 20.8 percent of GDP, just surpassing their 2000 peak.

Considerations in Setting Tax Policy

The primary aim of a tax system is to raise enough revenues to pay for government spending. Taxes vary, however, in their effects on individuals and on the economy as a whole. When choosing among tax policies, economists often evaluate the performance of a tax according to three criteria:

- Efficiency—the impact of the tax on economic activity;

- Equity—the fairness of a tax with respect to who bears its burden; and

- Simplicity—the costs of complying with and collecting the tax.

Because those criteria can conflict with each other, lawmakers often face difficult choices when setting tax policy.

Other considerations may also come into play. Many observers view the tax system as a means of achieving social policy goals—for example, by targeting tax hikes or tax preferences toward certain groups or activities. As a result, the current U.S. tax system contains many provisions whose main

Percentage of Tax Increase Needed to Achieve a Balanced Budget

	2011 President's Budget (OMB)	2011 CBO Baseline	2015 President's Budget (OMB)	2015 CBO Baseline
Increase All Taxes	59%	65%	17%	15%
Increase Income and Social Insurance Taxes	72%	78%	21%	18%
Increase Individual Income Taxes Only	141%	145%	37%	30%

Source: CRS calculations based on data from CBO's "Budget and Economic Outlook: Fiscal Years 2011 to 2021," January 2011, and the President's FY2012 Budget (OMB).

TAKEN FROM: Molly F. Sherlock, "Reducing the Budget Deficit: Tax Policy Options," Congressional Research Service, April 26, 2011.

goal is to encourage certain types of desired behavior, such as buying health insurance, saving for retirement, or owning a home. Those goals can sometimes clash with the objective of raising revenues in an efficient, equitable, and simple manner.

The Effect of Taxes on Economic Activity

Taxes influence the economy by causing people to alter their behavior, which generally results in a less efficient allocation of resources. People can respond to taxes in several ways: by changing the timing of their activities (such as accelerating bonus payments or asset sales into a certain year if they think tax rates on earnings or capital gains will rise in future years); by adjusting the form of their activities (such as substituting tax-preferred fringe benefits for cash wages if the tax rate on wages goes up); or by changing more fundamental aspects of their behavior (such as choosing to work or save less if tax rates on earnings or capital income rise).

Those behavioral changes occur because taxes raise the price of taxed activities and thereby lower the relative prices of other things. In particular, the individual income tax and payroll taxes reduce the returns from working (after-tax wages), which increases the return from other activities relative to working. Those taxes also reduce the returns from saving (the after-tax rate of return), which lowers the price of spending now relative to saving to spend in the future.

One measure of the effect of taxes on the returns from working and saving is the marginal tax rate—the tax paid per dollar of extra earnings or extra income from saving. . . . Following a reduction in income tax rates in 1986, the marginal tax rate for a representative family has remained at about 30 percent.

Changes in marginal tax rates have two different types of effects on people. On the one hand, the lower those tax rates are, the greater the share of the returns from additional work or saving that people can keep, thus encouraging them to

work and save more. On the other hand, because lower marginal tax rates increase after-tax income, they make it easier
for people to attain their consumption goals with a given
amount of work or saving, thus possibly causing people to
work and save less. On balance, the evidence suggests that reducing tax rates boosts work and saving relative to what would
occur otherwise, if budget deficits remain the same. But without other changes to taxes or spending, reducing tax rates
from current levels would generally decrease revenues and increase deficits; higher deficits, even with lower tax rates, can
reduce economic activity over the longer term.

Changes in marginal tax rates can also affect businesses—by encouraging them to alter the size and location of
investments or to engage in tax-avoidance activities (such as
shifting income from high-tax countries to low-tax countries
solely to reduce the amount of tax they owe worldwide). Many
observers have expressed concern that the U.S. corporate income tax hampers competitiveness because its top statutory
rate (35 percent) is one of the highest among countries in the
Organisation for Economic Co-operation and Development.
Those statutory rates, however, do not reflect differences
among various countries' tax bases and rate structures and
thus do not indicate the actual tax rates that multinational
companies face.

Some features of the tax code affect the economy by sub-
sidizing certain types of activities. Those subsidies often take
the form of special exclusions, exemptions, or deductions
from gross income; preferential tax rates; special tax credits
that offset tax liabilities (the amount people owe); or deferrals
of tax liabilities. Such subsidies are referred to as "tax expenditures," and their costs to the federal government are measured
in terms of forgone revenues, which total hundreds of billions
of dollars each year. According to estimates by the staff of the
Joint Committee on Taxation, the three largest tax expenditures in income tax law are the ones that provide preferential

treatment for employment-based health insurance, retirement savings, and home ownership. Each of those tax expenditures may help achieve certain societal goals: a healthier population, adequate financial resources for retirement, and stable communities of homeowners. But uncapped tax expenditures may also encourage overconsumption of the favored good or subsidize activity that would have taken place without the tax incentives. For example, those three income tax expenditures may prompt people to consume more health services than are necessary, reallocate existing savings from accounts that are not tax-preferred to retirement accounts, and acquire mortgages and purchase homes beyond their needs.

The Tax Burden and Who Bears It

Households generally bear the economic cost, or burden, of the taxes that they pay themselves, such as individual income taxes and employees' share of payroll taxes. But households also bear the burden of the taxes paid by businesses. In the judgment of CBO and most economists, the employers' share of payroll taxes is passed on to employees in the form of lower wages. In addition, households bear the burden of corporate income taxes, although the extent to which they do so as owners of capital, as workers, or as consumers is not clear.

One measure of the tax burden on households is the average tax rate—that is, taxes paid as a share of income. Federal taxes are progressive, meaning that average tax rates generally rise with income. In 2007, households in the bottom one-fifth (quintile) of the income distribution (those with an average income of $18,400, under a broad definition of income) paid about 4 percent of their income in federal taxes; those in the middle quintile, with an average income of $64,500, paid 14 percent; and those in the highest quintile, with an average income of $264,700, paid 25 percent. Average tax rates continued to rise within the highest quintile. Households in the top 1 percent of the income distribution faced an average tax rate of about 30 percent.

Much of the progressivity of the federal tax system derives from the largest source of revenues, the individual income tax, for which average tax rates rise with income. The next largest source of revenues, social insurance taxes, has average tax rates that vary little across most income groups—although the average rate is lower for higher-income households, because earnings above a certain threshold are not subject to the Social Security payroll tax and because earnings are a smaller portion of total income for that group. The average social insurance tax rate is higher than the average individual income tax rate for all income quintiles except the highest one. . . .

Approaches to Increasing Revenues

Although revenues are projected to reach historically high levels as a percentage of GDP by 2021, there are various reasons why lawmakers may want to consider options that would raise revenues. First, those anticipated levels may not be reached. CBO's projections of revenue growth assume that current laws remain unchanged. . . .

Lawmakers could raise revenues by modifying existing taxes—either by increasing tax rates or by expanding tax bases (the measures on which assessments of tax liabilities are made). Alternatively, they could impose new taxes on income, consumption, or particular activities. All of those approaches would have consequences not only for the amount of revenue collected but also for economic activity, tax burdens, and the complexity of the tax system.

An advantage of raising tax rates is that such a change would be simpler to implement than many of the alternative approaches to boosting revenues. Unlike other types of changes, an increase in rates generally does not require new reporting requirements, additional instructions, and more tax forms. However, as explained above, raising marginal tax rates would cause people and businesses to change their behavior in ways that affect economic activity. Raising rates would also have implications for the progressivity of the tax system, although those implications would depend on the types of taxes and taxpayers affected.

> *"With higher taxes, even entrepreneurs who do not care about personal gains will find it harder to grow through re-investment, raising external capital, and attracting new talent."*

Raising Taxes Will Not Resolve the Budget Deficit

Tino Sanandaji and Arvid Malm

Tino Sanandaji is an affiliated researcher at the Research Institute of Industrial Economics, and Arvid Malm is chief economist of the Swedish Taxpayers' Association. In the following viewpoint, they contend that tax increases on the rich are not a solution to budget deficits, and there is ample evidence that tax increases on the rich will hurt the economy. The amount of revenue collected from tax increases, the authors declare, is completely insufficient to either support planned spending or make a dent in the deficit. They point out that the economic successes attributed to tax increases under President Bill Clinton are really the result of a number of other factors unrelated to taxes. Higher taxes, the authors contend, adversely affect business owners' ability to grow their enterprises and create jobs. Rather than cut taxes, they conclude, the United States should close tax loopholes and increase the number of taxpayers.

Tino Sanandaji and Arvid Malm, "Obama's Folly: Why Taxing the Rich Is No Solution," *The American*, August 16, 2011. http://www.american.com/archive/2011/august/obamasfollytaxingtherich/article_print. Copyright © 2011 by the American Enterprise Institute. All rights reserved. Reproduced by permission.

As you read, consider the following questions:

1. According to the authors, how much revenue is expected to be raised over the next decade as a result of abolishing the Bush tax cuts for those who earn more than $250,000?

2. What percentage of the income of the highest earning 1 percent of Americans is entrepreneurial income, according to the viewpoint?

3. What portion of national income do the authors say is included in the basis for taxable income?

During the last three decades, the wealthy in America have become wealthier yet. American capitalists today are richer than virtually any other group in any country at any point in history. At the same time, the United States is experiencing record deficits, which threaten to bring the economy to its knees.

It is therefore hardly surprising that the solution proposed by some is to raise taxes on the rich. President [Barack] Obama has proposed doing so. Investing giant Warren Buffett made the case for taxing the wealthy this week [August 15, 2011] in the *New York Times*.

In one respect, Obama and Buffett are completely right. The rich do not "need" to pay lower taxes, and can certainly "afford" tax increases. If raising taxes on the rich would solve the deficit without hurting the economy, we would support the president's tax policy in a heartbeat. It would certainly be a more equitable solution to lower the already astounding standard of living of hedge fund owners than to "cut some kids off from getting a college scholarship."

Raising Taxes Is a Purely Symbolic Strategy

Unfortunately, the choices faced by America are not that simple. An economic strategy founded on raising taxes on the rich is based on two false premises. The first is that tax increases on the rich are a solution to current budget deficits. The second is the argument often put forward that there is "no evidence" that tax increases on the rich hurt the economy.

If you look carefully, President Obama has never explicitly stated that taxing the rich will bring in much revenue. Instead, the president has made sure to give voters the impression that the Republican refusal to tax the rich is the main cause of the deficit and thus the main obstacle to solving the fiscal crisis. For instance, Obama stated that "tax cuts that went to every millionaire and billionaire in the country" will "force us to borrow an average of $500 billion every year over the next decade." This message has been widely repeated: [Comedian and TV host] Jon Stewart, for instance, has assured his impressionable audience that without the [President George W.] Bush tax cuts, future deficits would not be a major problem.

But how much revenue are we really talking about? According to the *New York Times*, the president's plan to abolish the Bush tax cuts for those making more than $250,000 is expected to bring in merely $0.7 trillion over the next decade, or about 0.4 percent of gross domestic product [GDP] per year. As a comparison, the Congressional Budget Office estimates that the deficit over the same period is going to be $13 trillion, more than 6 percent of GDP per year.

The rich in America obviously have lots of money, but there are simply not enough of them to fund the president's preferred level of spending. For all the attention it has received, President Obama's "taxing the rich" policy can best be described as symbolic in nature, a rounding error compared to the deficits in the president's budget. Obama centers his speeches around tax hikes on the rich to lead voters into believing that hard choices on the economy can be avoided simply by taxing the rich at a higher rate.

Taxes and Entrepreneurs

Although the proposed tax increases will barely make a dent in the deficit, raising the top tax rates is likely to harm economic output. Many are convinced that tax increases have little or no damaging impact on the economy. We hear over and over again that notions of damaging effects from higher taxes are merely based on "trickle down" theory, which has been proven false.

This is not true. There exists robust empirical evidence that taxes impede economic activity. In conventional economics, only the magnitude of the negative impact of taxes on economic output is debated, not the existence of such an effect.

Let us focus on one such negative impact, the effect of taxes on the activity of business owners, an important segment of the economy. Business owners account for 40 percent of American capital, while firms with less than 500 employees employ half the private sector workforce.

The argument that taxes do not negatively affect small- and medium-size business tends to rely on a number of fallacies. One example is an article by [University of California,] Berkeley economics professor Laura Tyson, a member of Obama's advisory board, which was published in the *New York Times*. In the article, she claims that "the relationship between tax rates and economic activity, even though it has superficial appeal, is not supported by the evidence."

The most common fallacy repeated by Tyson is that taxes do not matter because the economy was booming during the [President Bill] Clinton years even though taxes went up. But tax increases are not the only economic event associated with the Clinton years, and therefore cannot be claimed to cause all events that took place in his presidency. The Clinton years also contained entry into NAFTA [North American Free Trade Agreement], welfare reform, and recovery from the 1992 recession. Most importantly though, the Clinton years included the IT [information technology] boom, which dramatically raised productivity growth in the United States as well as in other developed countries. It would strain the imagination to believe that Clinton's moderate marginal tax increase somehow caused the PC [personal computer] and Internet revolution.

Instead of picking one historic event that happens to fit your preferred theory, a more reasonable approach is to investigate all historical periods where taxes increased or decreased. This has been done by former Obama advisor Christina Romer and her husband David Romer. They also take into account the causes of tax increases. They find that tax increases tend to reduce economic growth, stating that "tax increases appear to have a very large, sustained, and highly significant negative impact on output," as "an exogenous tax increase of one percent of GDP lowers real GDP by almost three percent." Similar results have been obtained by Harvard economist Alberto Alesina using a different methodology.

Regarding small business, Tyson claims that "98 percent of small business owners will not be affected if the Bush tax cuts for these brackets expire." This is true, but also irrelevant. The United States has more than 25 million registered firms and more than 10 million self-employed. Most registered firms have zero employees and virtually no revenue, and exist for tax or legal reasons. Similarly, most self-employed businesses are small scale and employ no one other than the owner. What we are primarily concerned about is the impact of higher taxes on the small number of economically important firms. These are firms that collect sizable revenue, employ others and have the potential to grow and hire more workers. The owners of such firms are obviously far richer than the typical self-employed person, and are far more likely to be hit by tax increases on higher incomes or on capital gains.

Increasing Taxes Does Not Increase Revenue or Reduce Deficits

Everybody thinks that if you raise the marginal tax rates, you will bring in more revenue. But the taxpayers, workers, and investors of this country are smarter than we are. We've had a 93 percent marginal tax rate—then 70 percent, 50 percent, 30 percent, 40 percent and now a 35 percent marginal tax rate. But, regardless of the rate, we get the same amount of revenue. Higher tax rates just provide incentives for taxpayers to invest and earn money in ways that result in the least amount of taxes paid.

In other words, taxpayers have decided they are going to give us politicians in Washington just so much of their money to spend.

"Grassley: Tax Increases Don't Reduce Deficits,"
Newsmax, *July 12, 2011. www.newsmax.com.*

Implications for the Wider Economy

According to the "World Top Incomes Database," 28 percent of the income of the highest earning 1 percent of Americans, the group targeted by the president's tax hikes and the group most likely to own successful firms, is constituted by entrepreneurial income. This has implications for the wider economy. Following the 1986 tax reform, Princeton professor Harvey Rosen and coauthors investigated the effect of the personal income tax of business owners on their hiring activity. Business owners who received larger tax cuts expanded their hiring more.

This runs contrary to a common argument that taxes may matter for ordinary people, but not for the already rich or for entrepreneurs who care mainly about developing their company. Arianna Huffington, for example, has ridiculed the notion that the rich would care about and be affected by a few percentage points of higher taxes.

In fact, two groups that are consistently found to be *more* responsive to taxes than average are precisely the self-employed and high-income earners. Both groups can more easily evade taxes and tend to have more control over their economic behavior. Looking at historic American tax reforms, economists Jonathan Gruber and Emmanuel Saez demonstrate that increases in taxes reduce taxable income especially for high-income earners.

We might like to believe that someone who is already a millionaire doesn't care about obtaining even more money. But this does not appear to be how actual millionaires behave. Even some billionaires actively attempt to lower their tax rates, for example by relocating to tax havens.

While excessive acquisitiveness (greed) is hardly a virtue, acquisitiveness and ambition might not be bad traits in entrepreneurs. Otherwise Steve Jobs, Sam Walton, and Warren Buffett might have cashed out and retired in Tahiti after making their first $100 million instead of staying on and developing their companies. . . .

One way to better approximate the behavior of innovative entrepreneurs is to study investments in the venture capital (VC) sector. VC plays a central role for high-potential firms. More than half of those entrepreneurial firms that were successful enough to make an IPO [initial public offering] and become public had VC backing. Harvard researchers Josh Lerner and Paul Gompers show that VC fund-raising in the United States is highly sensitive to capital gains taxes. Their results indicate that the cause for this is that lower capital gains taxes encourage more skilled individuals to become entrepreneurs. . . .

Another common fallacy in the tax debate is that entrepreneurs do not care about taxes because they are motivated by intrinsic factors. Indeed, nonmonetary rewards are important for entrepreneurs (although three-quarters self-report that they also care about monetary rewards). But taxes also matter for the ability to build a new company, even disregarding the personal wealth of the entrepreneur.

Profit taxes lower the amount of capital available for reinvestment. The negative effect of corporate income taxes on business investments has been confirmed by numerous studies, such as a recent one conducted by Harvard economist Andrei Shleifer and coauthors.

Furthermore, the growth of new high-potential ventures depends not only on individual entrepreneurs, but also on the ability to attract talented employees. Like entrepreneurs, these workers often have high paying and rewarding jobs, and a career ladder that they must leave if they choose to work for the new company. Few early stage entrepreneurial firms can compete on wages, instead relying on option programs and promises of future reward. Such incentive mechanisms are made more costly by high taxes, which disproportionally target the small probability of great success.

With higher taxes, even entrepreneurs who do not care about personal gains will find it harder to grow through reinvestment, raising external capital, and attracting new talent. In short, even if you don't care about taxes, taxes care about you.

What to Do About the Tax Code

The United States still leads Western Europe in innovative entrepreneurship. For instance, each year venture capital investments per person are about four to five times higher in the United States than in Western Europe. Is the president willing to risk one of the last sectors in which the United States enjoys a comparative advantage, betting that less burdensome taxes have nothing to do with this competitive edge?

If the tax increases on capitalists proposed by President Obama would balance the budget, perhaps we should endure the damaging effect on economic output. However, as noted above, the impact on the deficit is symbolic in nature. Rather, the motivation appears to be political, a combination of resentment towards the rich and a reaction to excessively ideological supply-siders.

Currently, less than half of national income is included in the basis for taxable income. Instead of raising tax rates, we can close tax loopholes and broaden the tax base so as to raise revenue to its historic average, while controlling federal spending. This is preferable to increasing tax rates based on the faulty notion that raising taxes on the rich does not hurt economic output.

> *"Limiting total tax expenditures could produce enough revenue to achieve very substantial cuts in future budget deficits while also lowering personal tax rates."*

Placing Limits on Tax Expenditures Will Raise Revenue and Lower the Budget Deficit

Martin Feldstein

Martin Feldstein is a professor of economics at Harvard University, and he was chairman of the Council of Economic Advisers from 1982–1984. In this viewpoint, he explains tax expenditures and how limiting them is critical to dealing with the deficit. Tax expenditures, Feldstein explains, are tax credits given to taxpayers on items such as mortgage interest or allowing taxpayers to pay no taxes on employer-provided health care benefits. He illustrates how these tax expenditures are erroneously calculated as tax cuts in budget calculations, and he argues that limiting these expenditures would result in a decrease in spending but not an

Martin Feldstein, "Another Way to Curb Deficits," *Weekly Standard*, vol. 16. no. 35, May 30, 2011. http://www.weeklystandard.com/articles/another-way-curb-deficits_567617 .html. Copyright © 2011 by the Weekly Standard. All rights reserved. Reproduced by permission.

increase in taxes. He concludes that limiting tax expenditures will ultimately lower personal tax rates because Congress will not need to introduce new or higher taxes in the future to generate revenue.

As you read, consider the following questions:

1. What does Feldstein say is a $1.4 trillion subsidy to health insurance disguised as a tax reduction?

2. What, according to Feldstein, must voters believe is true of all taxpayers in order to make them support limits on tax expenditures?

3. How much of his $3,000 per year mortgage interest would a taxpayer with a 15 percent marginal tax rate have to pay if expenditures were limited, according to Feldstein?

President [Barack] Obama is increasing government spending even faster than the budget numbers imply. That's because some of his increased spending is disguised as cuts in taxes.

When the government gives a tax credit to homeowners who buy solar energy panels, it's just like giving them a cash subsidy to buy those panels. But it's recorded as a reduction in taxes rather than as an increase in outlays.

Similarly, when the president calls for an increase in the child care credit, that's also treated as a tax cut rather than the rise in spending that it actually is.

According to calculations of the Treasury Department that are hidden deep in the government's annual budget, there are hundreds of billions of dollars of spending every year that are recorded as tax reductions. The biggest of these "tax expenditures," as they are called, is the exclusion of employer health insurance premiums from the taxable income of employees. That exclusion resulted in a tax reduction of $160 billion in

2010 and is projected to be $1.4 trillion between 2010 and 2016. That's a $1.4 trillion subsidy to health insurance that is disguised as a tax reduction.

Limiting total tax expenditures could produce enough revenue to achieve very substantial cuts in future budget deficits while also lowering personal tax rates. Indeed, if tax expenditures are not reduced, Congress will eventually be forced to raise tax rates or to introduce new taxes. That's because there is no way to achieve the needed reductions in future deficits just by cutting traditional government outlays, even if there are further cuts in defense spending. And slowing the growth of Social Security and Medicare is needed just to avoid an explosion of future spending on those programs.

Limiting tax expenditures should have bipartisan appeal. Republicans should welcome limits on tax expenditures as a way to cut hidden government spending. Democrats should accept it as a way to raise the revenue that they insist must be part of any deficit reduction plan. And as I will explain below, it is also a natural way to achieve an automatic "fail safe" mechanism to make sure that deficits decline as promised.

Limiting Expenditures Is Not a Tax Increase

Although limiting the use of tax expenditures would produce additional tax revenue, it is very different from other possible revenue increases. It doesn't raise marginal tax rates, doesn't discourage work or entrepreneurship, and doesn't tax saving and risk taking. It is really a reduction in government spending, not a tax increase. And deep enough cuts in tax expenditures would actually allow reductions in personal tax rates as well as in budget deficits.

I am surprised that some conservatives who favor cutting government nondefense spending oppose limiting tax expenditures because they regard the resulting increase in tax revenue as a tax increase. That fails to distinguish between the accounting effect of cutting tax expenditures and the eco-

What Are Tax Expenditures, and What Are Their Effects?

Tax expenditures are revenue losses attributable to tax provisions that often result from the use of the tax system to promote social goals without incurring direct expenditures. How tax expenditures are structured affects both who will benefit from them and how much they will reduce federal revenues.

Income tax provisions generally seek to promote one or more of three broad objectives: measuring income accurately, distributing fiscal benefits and burdens based on a household's ability to pay, and promoting activities or behaviors that are considered socially desirable. . . .

Tax expenditures can take many forms. Some result from tax provisions that reduce the present value of taxable income through deferral allowances, or special exclusions, exemptions, or deductions from gross income. Others affect a household's after-tax income more directly through tax credits or preferential rates for specific activities.

Urban Institute and Brookings Institution, "Tax Expenditures: What Are They and How Are They Structured?," The Tax Policy Briefing Book: A Citizens' Guide for the 2008 Election and Beyond, Tax Policy Center, 2008.

nomic effect. Although government accounting rules treat the end of a tax credit or the limit of a tax deduction as a revenue increase, the economic effect is the same as a cut in spending. Anyone who favors less government spending should also favor cutting tax expenditures.

At a personal level, reductions in tax expenditures would be unpopular with those who see their own benefits reduced.

That's true of any form of spending cut, whether through the tax code or the outlay side of the budget. But voters who recognize the seriousness of the deficit situation may nevertheless support a limit to tax expenditures if they believe that all taxpayers are being asked to accept a sacrifice.

That's why I think that putting a cap on the total value of tax reductions that each individual can achieve through tax expenditures is better than those plans that would limit only a few of the tax deductions. More specifically, I favor limiting the tax reduction that individuals can achieve through itemized deductions and the exclusion of employer health insurance payments to 2 percent of each taxpayer's adjusted gross income. Such a cap would allow each taxpayer to benefit from all of the current tax rules but would limit the total resulting tax reduction to no more than 2 percent of that taxpayer's total income.

Note that the limit applies to the resulting tax reductions and not to the deductions themselves. A taxpayer with a 15 percent marginal tax rate who pays mortgage interest of $3,000 a year would have to count 15 percent of that $3,000, or $450, toward his allowable cap.

> *"If the rich were taxed at the same rates they were half a century ago, they'd be paying ... enough to accomplish everything the nation needs while also reducing future deficits."*

Tax Increases for Wealthy Americans Would Greatly Reduce the Deficit

Robert Reich

Robert Reich is chancellor's professor of public policy at the University of California, Berkeley. In the following viewpoint, Reich insists that raising taxes on the wealthiest Americans is the only way to fund vital government services and reduce budget deficits. No other approach to raising revenue or cutting spending, Reich maintains, would be sufficient. Further, he points out, working-class families' taxes have gone up considerably during the last few decades—even while their incomes have dropped—while the wealthiest Americans' taxes have dropped by more than half.

As you read, consider the following questions:

1. How much, on average, have the bottom 90 percent of Americans' wages gone up compared to thirty years ago, according to Reich?

Robert Reich, "Deficit Won't Budge Without Raising Taxes on the Rich," *Christian Science Monitor*, April 5, 2011. http://www.csmonitor.com/Business/Robert-Reich/2011/0405/Deficit-won-t-budge-without-raising-taxes-on-the-rich. Copyright © 2011 by Robert Reich. All rights reserved. Reproduced by permission.

2. What was the top 1 percent's share of national income in 1981, according to the viewpoint?

3. What, according to Reich, was the estate tax percentage in 2000?

It's tax time. It's also a time when right-wing Republicans are setting the agenda for massive spending cuts that will hurt most Americans.

Here's the truth: The only way America can reduce the long-term budget deficit, maintain vital services, protect Social Security and Medicare, invest more in education and infrastructure, and not raise taxes on the working middle class is by raising taxes on the superrich.

Other Approaches to Raising Revenue Fall Short

Even if we got rid of corporate welfare subsidies for big oil, big agriculture, and big Pharma—even if we cut back on our bloated defense budget—it wouldn't be nearly enough.

The vast majority of Americans can't afford to pay more. Despite an economy that's twice as large as it was thirty years ago, the bottom 90 percent are still stuck in the mud. If they're employed, they're earning on average only about $280 more a year than thirty years ago adjusted for inflation. That's less than a 1 percent gain over more than a third of a century. (Families are doing somewhat better but that's only because so many families now have to rely on two incomes.)

Middle-Class Taxes Are Up, Upper-Class Taxes Are Down

Yet even as their share of the nation's total income has withered, the tax burden on the middle has grown. Today's working and middle-class taxpayers are shelling out a bigger chunk of income in payroll taxes, sales taxes, and property taxes than thirty years ago.

Raising Taxes on the Rich Would Be True Shared Sacrifice

While the poor and middle class fight for us in Afghanistan, and while most Americans struggle to make ends meet, we mega-rich continue to get our extraordinary tax breaks. . . .

My friends and I have been coddled long enough by a billionaire-friendly Congress. It's time for our government to get serious about shared sacrifice.

Warren E. Buffett, "Stop Coddling the Super-Rich,"
New York Times, *August 14, 2011.*

It's just the opposite for superrich.

The top 1 percent's share of national income has doubled over the past three decades (from 10 percent in 1981 to well over 20 percent now). The richest one-tenth of 1 percent's share has tripled. And they're doing better than ever. According to a new analysis by the *Wall Street Journal*, total compensation and benefits at publicly traded Wall Street banks and securities firms hit a record in 2010—$135 billion. That's up 5 percent from 2009.

Yet, remarkably, taxes on the top have plummeted. From the 1940s until 1980, the top tax income tax rate on the highest earners in America was at least 70 percent. In the 1950s, it was 91 percent. Now it's 35 percent. Even if you include deductions and credits, the rich are now paying a far lower share of their incomes in taxes than at any time since World War II.

The estate tax (which only hits the top 2 percent) has also been slashed. In 2000 it was 55 percent and kicked in after $1 million. Today it's 35 percent and kicks in at $5 million. Capi-

tal gains—comprising most of the income of the superrich—
were taxed at 35 percent in the late 1980s. They're now taxed
at 15 percent.

If the rich were taxed at the same rates they were half a
century ago, they'd be paying over $350 billion more this year
[2011] alone, which translates into trillions over the next decade. That's enough to accomplish everything the nation needs
while also reducing future deficits.

> *"In 2009, states overestimated their revenues by more than $50 billion, due largely to the unexpected falloff in personal income taxes."*

The Price of Taxing the Rich

Robert Frank

Robert Frank is the wealth reporter for the Wall Street Journal *and author of* Richistan: A Journey Through the American Wealth Boom and the Lives of the New Rich *and* The High-Beta Rich: How the Manic Wealthy Will Take Us to the Next Boom, Bubble, and Bust. *In the following viewpoint, he argues that the income of the wealthy has become increasingly unstable, making it risky for government to rely on tax revenue from the rich to repair the deficit. Frank reports on the hardships endured by states that have made the mistake of relying too heavily on tax revenue from a few high-income earners whose incomes are largely tied to the stock market, which is and will remain highly volatile. States must take volatility into consideration when planning budgets, the viewpoint illustrates, to avoid severe shortfalls in revenue that have plagued states in the past. Because predicting the stock market's activity is impossible, Frank reports, states must not rely so heavily on income that is largely dependent on this activity.*

Robert Frank, "The Price of Taxing the Rich," *Wall Street Journal*, March 26, 2011. Copyright © 2011 by Dow Jones Inc. All rights reserved. Reproduced by permission.

As you read, consider the following questions:

1. Which states does Frank say are the most heavily reliant on tax revenue from the wealthy?

2. What percentage of federal taxes was paid by the top 1 percent of wage earners in 2008, according to the viewpoint?

3. According to Brad Williams's 2005 report cited in the viewpoint, by how much could California's state income tax revenues vary in a single year?

The top 1% of earners fill the coffers of states like California and New York during a boom—and leave them starved for revenue in a bust.

As Brad Williams walked the halls of the California state capitol in Sacramento on a recent afternoon, he spotted a small crowd of protesters battling state spending cuts. They wore shiny white buttons that said "We Love Jobs!" and argued that looming budget reductions will hurt the Golden State's working class.

Mr. Williams shook his head. "They're missing the real problem," he said.

The working class may be taking a beating from spending cuts used to close a cavernous deficit, Mr. Williams said, but the root of California's woes is its reliance on taxing the wealthy.

Nearly half of California's income taxes before the recession came from the top 1% of earners: households that took in more than $490,000 a year. High earners, it turns out, have especially volatile incomes—their earnings fell by more than twice as much as the rest of the population's during the recession. When they crashed, they took California's finances down with them.

Mr. Williams, a former economic forecaster for the state, spent more than a decade warning state leaders about

California's overdependence on the rich. "We created a revenue cliff," he said. "We built a large part of our government on the state's most unstable income group."

New York, New Jersey, Connecticut and Illinois—states that are the most heavily reliant on the taxes of the wealthy—are now among those with the biggest budget holes. A large population of rich residents was a blessing during the boom, showering states with billions in tax revenue. But it became a curse as their incomes collapsed with financial markets.

Arriving at a time of greatly increased public spending, this reversal highlights the dependence of the states on the outsize incomes of the wealthy. The result for state finances and budgets has been extreme volatility.

In New York before the recession, the top 1% of earners, who made more than $580,000 a year, paid 41% of the state's income taxes in 2007, up from 25% in 1994, according to state tax data. The top 1% of taxpayers paid 40% or more of state income taxes in New Jersey and Connecticut. In Illinois, which has a flat income-tax rate of 5%, the top 15% paid more than half the state's income taxes.

This growing dependence on wealthy taxpayers is being driven by soaring salaries at the top of the income ladder and by the nation's progressive income taxes, which levy the highest rates on the highest taxable incomes. The top federal income-tax rate has fallen dramatically over the past century, from more than 90% during World War II to 35% today. But the top tax rate—which applies to joint filers reporting $379,000 in taxable income—is still twice as high as the rate for joint filers reporting income of $69,000 or less.

The future of federal income taxes on the wealthy remains in flux. The top tax rate is 35%, following the congressional tax battle last year. But in 2013, the rate is scheduled to go back to 39.6% unless Congress takes further action.

State income taxes are generally less progressive than federal income taxes, and more than a half dozen states have no income tax. Yet a number of states have recently hiked taxes on the top earners to raise revenue during the recession. New York, for instance, imposed a "millionaire's tax" in 2009 on those earning $500,000 or more, although the tax is expected to expire at the end of 2011. Connecticut's top income-tax rate has crept up to 6.5% from 4.5% in 2002, while Oregon raised the top tax rate to 11% from 9% for filers with income of more than $500,000.

As they've grown, the incomes of the wealthy have become more unstable. Between 2007 and 2008, the incomes of the top-earning 1% fell 16%, compared to a decline of 4% for U.S. earners as a whole, according to the IRS. Because today's highest salaries are usually linked to financial markets—through stock-based pay or investments—they are more prone to sudden shocks.

The income swings have created more extreme booms and busts for state governments. In New York, the top 1% of taxpayers contribute more to the state's year-to-year tax swings than all the other taxpayers combined, according to a study by the Rockefeller Institute of Government. In its January report downgrading New Jersey's credit rating, Standard & Poor's stated that New Jersey's wealth "translates into a high ability to pay taxes but might also contribute to potential revenue volatility."

State budget shortfalls have other causes, of course, from high unemployment and weak retail sales to falling real estate values and the rising costs of health care and pensions. State spending has expanded rapidly over the past decade. California's total spending grew from $99.2 billion in 2000–01 to a projected $136 billion in 2010–11, not including federal funds, according to the state Department of Finance. Though California's spending slipped by 15% during the recession, it has since returned to near prerecession levels.

Some states may get a lifeline this year from the financial markets. Starting late last year, California, New Jersey and others began seeing higher-than-expected income-tax revenues and capital gains revenues, suggesting the start of the next boom cycle. Still, because many states based their spending plans on the assumption that the windfalls from the wealthy would return every year, they are now grappling with multibillion-dollar shortfalls.

A recent study by the Pew Center on the States and the Rockefeller Institute found that in 2009, states overestimated their revenues by more than $50 billion, due largely to the unexpected falloff in personal income taxes. Sales and corporate taxes have also fallen, but they account for a much smaller share of tax revenue in many states.

Tax experts say the problems at the state level could spread to Washington, as the highest earners gain a larger share of both national income and the tax burden. The top 1% paid 38% of federal income taxes in 2008, up from 25% in 1991, and they earned 20% of all national income in 2008, up from 13% in 1991, according to the Tax Foundation.

"These revenues have a narcotic effect on legislatures," said Greg Torres, president of MassINC, a nonpartisan think tank. "They become numb to the trend and think the revenue picture is improving, but they don't realize the money is ephemeral."

Kicking the addiction has proven difficult, since it's so fraught with partisan politics. Republicans advocate lowering taxes on the wealthy to broaden state tax bases and reduce volatility. Democrats oppose the move, saying a less progressive tax system would only add to growing income inequality.

In a blog post called "The Volatility Monster," California Democratic State Sen. Noreen Evans wrote that "the true response to solving the volatility problem is to make sure Californians are fully employed and decently paid. Preserving the state's progressive tax system is fundamental to combating the rising riches at the top and rising poverty at the bottom. Flattening our tax system would simply increase this already historic income inequality," she wrote.

U.S. Rep. Tom McClintock (R., Calif.) has for years advocated a flat tax in California to reduce volatility and keep high earners from leaving the state. "California has one of the most steeply disproportionate income taxes in the nation," he said. "A flatter, broader tax rate would help stabilize the most volatile of California's revenues."

Rainy-day funds, which can help bail out governments during recessions, have also run into political opposition or proven too small to save state budgets. A study by the Center on Budget and Policy Priorities found that effective rainy-day funds should be 15% of state operating expenditures—more than three times the state average before the crisis. Massachusetts, which saw a 75% drop in capital gains collections during the recession, won plaudits from ratings firms and economists for creating a rainy-day fund in 2010 using future capital gains revenues.

Economists and state budget chiefs say the best hedge is better planning. Budget staffers in New York, for instance, now spend more time studying Wall Street pay and bonuses to more accurately predict state revenues. The state's budget director avoids overly optimistic forecasts based on a previous year's strong growth.

"We're glad we have the revenue from the wealthy, and we want to encourage these people to stay and prosper," said Robert L. Megna, budget director for New York State. "But we have to recognize that because you have them, you'll have this big volatility."

The story of Mr. Williams, the former chief economist and forecaster for the California Legislative Analyst's Office, shows just how vulnerable states have become to the income shocks among the rich, and why reform has proven difficult.

In the mid-1990s, shortly after taking the job, Mr. Williams discovered he had a problem. Part of his job was to help state politicians plan their budgets and tax projections.

A lanky, 6-foot-4-inch 58-year-old, with piercing blue eyes and a fondness for cycling, Mr. Williams prided himself on his deep data dives. The *Wall Street Journal* named him California's most accurate forecaster in 1998 for his work the prior decade. He and his team placed a special focus on employment and age data and developed their own econometric models to make improvements.

Historically, California's tax revenues tracked the broader state economy. Yet in the mid-1990s, Mr. Williams noticed that they had started to diverge. Employment was barely growing while income-tax revenue was soaring.

"It was like we suddenly had two different economies," Mr. Williams said. "There was the California economy and then there were personal income taxes."

In all his years of forecasting, he had rarely encountered such a puzzle. He did some economic sleuthing and discovered that most of the growth was coming from a small group of high earners. The average incomes of the top 20% of Californian earners (households making $95,000 in 1998) jumped by an inflation-adjusted 75% between 1980 and 1998, while incomes for the rest of the state grew by less than 3% over the same period. Capital gains realizations—largely stock sales—quadrupled between 1994 and 1999, to nearly $80 billion.

Mr. Williams reported his findings in early 2000, in a report called "California's Changing Income Distribution," which was widely circulated in the state capital. He wrote that state tax collections would be "subject to more volatility than in the past."

Mr. Williams wasn't the only one noticing the state's dependence on the wealthy. Economists and governors had for years lamented the state's high tax rates on the rich, and in 2009 a bipartisan commission set up by then Gov. Arnold

Schwarzenegger recommended an across-the-board reduction in income-tax rates and a broader sales tax to reduce the state's dependence on the wealthy. The income-tax rate on Californians making more than $1 million a year is 10.3%, compared to less than 6% for those making under $26,600. Combined with the rising share of income going to the top, the state's progressive rates amplify the impact of the income gains or losses of the wealthy.

California's dependence on income taxes has also grown because of its shifting economy. Income taxes now account for more than half of its general revenue, up from about a third in 1981. Because the state's sales and use tax applies mainly to goods, rather than faster growing services, it has declined in importance. The state's corporate tax has also shrunk relative to income taxes because of tax credits and other changes.

By the late 1990s, Mr. Williams realized that his job had changed. California's future was no longer tied to the broader economy, but to a small group of ultra-earners. To predict the state's revenue, he had to start forecasting the fortunes of the rich. That meant forecasting the performance of stocks—specifically, a handful of high-tech stocks.

He pored over SEC filings for Apple, Oracle and other California tech giants. He met with the financial advisers to the rich, asking them about the investment plans of their clients. He watched daily stock movements and stock sales reported by the state's tax collectors.

Working with the state's tax collectors, he did a geographic breakdown of capital gains. The vast majority were in Silicon Valley.

"We knew there was a bubble," he said, "We just didn't know when it would fall, or by how much."

After the dot-com bust, the state's revenues from capital gains fell by more than two-thirds, to $5 billion in 2003 from $17 billion in 2001, while personal income taxes fell 15% over the same period. The recession created a mirror image of the boom, with the wealthy leading the crash and dragging tax revenues down with them. By 2002, California had a budget shortfall of more than $20 billion.

The deficit lingered for years, but its lessons seemed to be quickly forgotten in the state capital. By 2005, California was enjoying another surge in spending fed by the incomes of the wealthy.

Mr. Williams started warning of another government crisis. In 2005, he released a report stating that the state's tax revenues could vary by as much as $6 billion in a single year, and that such swings were "more likely than not." He recommended several potential reforms, including flatter income-tax rates, "income averaging," which allows the wealthy to spread their tax payments for unusual windfalls over a longer period of time, and a rainy-day fund.

His proposals failed to gain any traction with the legislature. Many Democrats refused to consider tax hikes on the middle class and lower rates for the rich. In 2009, voters rejected a proposed spending cap, which among other things, would have helped to create a rainy-day fund.

One of the leading advocates for such a fund is Roger Niello, a former Republican assemblyman who has long been among the top 1% of state earners. He and his family own a chain of luxury car dealerships, and during the recession, his income fell by more than half because of the decline of auto sales. Though he's still "fine financially," he said, his personal experience taught him that "people in this income group have the most variable incomes."

Darrell Steinberg, the Democratic leader of the state senate, agrees that the dependence on the wealthy is "one of our most fundamental problems." Yet he concedes that his own spending priorities—including a large expansion of mental health programs funded by a millionaire's tax—have added to the current mismatch between revenues and spending.

"I have no regrets given the number of people we've helped," he said. "But I guess you could say I did my part with spending."

As time went by, Mr. Williams became increasingly frustrated. To do his job properly, he had to predict the stock market. "And that's impossible," he said. He also felt that all of his research and warnings fell on deaf ears. In 2007, he decided to retire, and he now works for a consulting firm.

"I was a broken record," he said. "I just kept saying the same thing over and over. And with my job, there was no real pleasure in being right."

—Vauhini Vara contributed to this article.

| "*Tax reform is critical to rebuilding our economy to be stronger and more stable than in the past.*"

Tax Reform Is Necessary to Reduce the Deficit

Barack Obama

Barack Obama is the forty-fourth president of the United States and former US senator from Illinois. In the following viewpoint, he explains why tax reforms are necessary and how they will help lower the budget deficit. Tax rates can be lowered overall, Obama insists, if tax breaks and loopholes are eliminated so that all Americans are paying their fair share and not gaming the system to avoid payment. In addition, Obama asserts, by allowing unfair tax cuts to expire on wealthy Americans, the federal deficit can be reduced. In addition to tax reform, Obama maintains, the United States must increase job creation and economic growth. Obama concludes by supporting a principle proposed by billionaire Warren Buffett that postulates that American households making over $1 million a year should never pay a smaller share of their income in taxes than middle-class families pay.

Barack Obama, "Living Within Our Means and Investing in the Future: The President's Plan for Economic Growth and Deficit Reduction," Office of Management and Budget, September 2011.

As you read, consider the following questions:

1. According to President Obama, by how much would Americans have to agree to cut every program in the entire budget to reduce deficits and put the United States on a fiscally sustainable path without reforming taxes?

2. According to the viewpoint, what percentage of taxpayers must pay tax preparers to fill out their tax returns?

3. How much does President Obama say would be raised by allowing tax cuts enacted in 2001 and 2003 to expire?

The president is committed to reducing the deficit through a balanced approach—one that restrains spending across the budget, including in the tax code; asks the wealthiest among us to contribute to deficit reduction; and lays the foundation for future growth. That is why the president is calling on the Congress to undertake comprehensive tax reform to cut rates, cut inefficient tax breaks, cut the deficit, and increase jobs and growth in the United States—while observing the "Buffett Rule" [a principle that everyone should pay their fair share in taxes] that people making over $1 million should not pay lower taxes than the middle class.

Tax reform is critical to rebuilding our economy to be stronger and more stable than in the past. Two of our biggest economic challenges—creating jobs and reducing long-term deficits—both depend on a simpler, fairer, more progressive tax system than we have today.

The administration believes, like many others, that tax cuts play an important role in job creation. But the administration believes that broad tax cuts for the middle class—rather than for only the wealthiest one or two percent of Americans—are far more effective at creating jobs and growing the economy. When millions of middle-class families across the country have more money in their bank accounts to spend in their communities, businesses large and small can grow, innovate, invest, and hire. The success of the American economy has long been built on the vibrancy of our middle class, and our efforts to create a tax system that is fairer, simpler, and more progressive reflect that reality.

Tax Reform or Deep Cuts

Tax reform is also an important part of reducing our long-term deficits and placing our country on a fiscally sustainable path. We cannot address a deficit a decade in the making through spending cuts alone—that is, unless we, as a country, agree to cut every program in the entire budget by more than a quarter, including all defense spending, Social Security and Medicare benefits, and veterans' benefits, along with everything else. The administration believes in a balanced approach that cuts spending responsibly, but also asks the most well off in society—many of whom, through loopholes and other exemptions, pay less in taxes than most middle-class families—to contribute their fair share toward reducing the deficit and healing our economy.

Comprehensive Tax Reform Is Crucial

The tax code has become increasingly complicated and unfair. Changes enacted during the previous administration were skewed in favor of the wealthiest taxpayers and reduced the tax code's overall progressivity. Under today's tax laws, those who can afford expert advice can avoid paying their fair share and interests with the most connected lobbyists can get exemptions and special treatment written into our tax code. While many of the tax incentives serve important purposes, taken together the tax expenditures in the law are inefficient, unfair, duplicative, or even unnecessary. The corporate tax system provides special incentives for some industries, like oil and gas producers, yet fails to provide sufficient incentives for companies to invest in America. Because our corporate tax system is so riddled with special interest loopholes, our system has one of the highest statutory tax rates among developed countries to generate about the same amount of corporate tax revenue as our developed country partners as a share of our economy; this, in turn, hurts our competitiveness in the world economy. In addition, a large fraction of the tax code is now temporary and expires periodically, adding uncertainty for households and businesses, and complicating the fiscal outlook.

The result is a tax code that neither serves the American people nor our economy. Recent data show that the tax code places a relatively light tax burden on the wealthiest Americans. As [American businessman] Warren Buffett has pointed out, his effective tax rate is lower than his secretary's, although this is not true for many small business owners and others who primarily receive labor income. The tax code also places a substantial compliance burden on taxpayers. For instance, taxpayers filing Form 1040 spent an average of 21 hours preparing their returns and most taxpayers—about 60 percent— find themselves paying tax preparers to fill out their returns. We have not had a comprehensive reform of our tax code in a generation. The last time we had one, the Internet was a small tool used by researchers, the euro did not exist, and global supply chains and commerce were far less developed. The time has come for tax reform to modernize our tax code, make it fairer, and to reduce its complexity. . . .

Simplicity, Fairness, and Efficiency Are Key to Tax Reform

This will make our tax code simpler, fairer, and more efficient—and end a system that allows households making millions of dollars annually to pay lower tax rates than middle-class families.

This tax reform would make an important contribution as part of a balanced plan to reduce the deficit. For individuals,

Proposed Tax Expenditure Cuts and Reforms: Revenue Raised in Billions of Dollars

	2012	2013	2014	2015	2016	2017	2018	2019	2020	2012–2020
Restructure Tax Benefits for Low-Income Families, Families with Children, and Eliminate the Standard Deduction and Personal Exemption	-155	-209	-221	-213	-216	-221	-226	-230	-234	-1,914
Tax Capital Gains above $1,000 Exclusion	-1	2	5	29	38	40	42	44	46	243
Restructure Itemized Deductions and Eliminate Tax Expenditures	230	338	369	397	421	444	428	447	470	3,544

TAKEN FROM: Molly F. Sherlock, "Reducing the Budget Deficit: Tax Policy Options," Congressional Research Service, April 26, 2011.

the high-income tax cuts enacted in 2001 and 2003 would be allowed to expire and additional inefficient tax breaks would be cut to raise an additional $700 billion while observing the Buffett Rule and making the tax code fair for all Americans. For corporations, deficit neutral tax reform would make businesses pay for the cost of any of the roughly $300 billion in temporary tax breaks over the next decade that would be continued as part of the reform but have generally been deficit financed in the past, like the research and experimentation credit. Together, individuals and corporations would be contributing roughly proportionately to deficit reduction.

The president recognizes that comprehensive tax reform will take time and will not be easy. However, the president also believes that the joint committee must take action now that locks in improvements in our tax code that increase fairness and efficiency while helping put the nation on a sustainable fiscal course.

Closing Tax Loopholes Will Help Reduce the Deficit

To begin the national conversation about tax reform, the president is offering a detailed set of specific tax loophole closers and measures to broaden the tax base that, together with the expiration of the high-income tax cuts, would be more than sufficient to hit the $1.5 trillion target for tax reform and cut inefficient expenditures as well as move the tax system closer to observing the Buffett Rule. These measures include: cutting tax preferences for high-income households; eliminating special tax breaks for oil and gas companies; closing the carried interest loophole for investment fund managers; and eliminating benefits for those who buy corporate jets. It is incumbent on everyone who supports comprehensive tax reform to not only call for lower rates but to identify specific tax loopholes and tax expenditures that they would be willing to reform or eliminate as part of a reform effort. The president is making good on this commitment by putting forward a specific . . . set of tax expenditure reforms.

Tax reform should draw on items listed here, together with the elimination of additional inefficient tax breaks, to finance the reduction of marginal rates and comport with the Buffett Rule. If the joint committee is unable to undertake comprehensive tax reform, the president believes these measures should be enacted on a stand-alone basis. Although this would fall short of the president's five principles for reform, it would move the tax system closer to several of them.

This fallback of allowing the high-income tax cuts to expire, and enacting specific loophole closers and base broadeners, would lock in deficit reduction from tax changes that is as specific and certain as the deficit reduction coming from the president's proposed spending reductions, and would be a critical part of a balanced plan to put America on a course toward fiscal sustainability. This would significantly improve the country's fiscal standing, represent an important step toward more fundamentally transforming our tax code, and serve as a strong foundation for economic growth and job creation.

The measures that could contribute to comprehensive tax reform or, absent such reform, act as a backstop, include bringing fairness to the individual tax code, incorporating measures in the American Jobs Act, closing business loopholes and broadening the business tax base, eliminating fossil fuel preferences, reforming the treatment of insurance companies and products, reforming the U.S. international tax system, and other changes. These proposals would generally become effective on January 1, 2013.

"In this era of endless electioneering and political polarization, a bipartisan tax reform bill just seems a wistful dream."

Reducing the Deficit Through Tax Reform Is Unrealistic

Len Burman

Len Burman is an affiliated scholar at the Tax Policy Center (TPC), which he cofounded and directed until 2009. In the following viewpoint, he offers his opinion on why tax reform necessary to reduce the deficit cannot be accomplished. Burman recounts his involvement with the process of writing the Tax Reform Act of 1986, which passed with bipartisan support. In today's political climate, which Burman asserts is devoid of any bipartisan agreement, an effective tax reform proposal would have no chance of being implemented. In addition to the highly polarized political climate, he concludes, many of the reforms that were available in 1986 are no longer available because of changes imposed by previous laws. Despite the increased need for reform, he laments, the likelihood that it will take place is next to zero.

Len Burman, "Tax Reform Is Essential, Inevitable, and Impossible," *Christian Science Monitor*, October 21, 2011. http://www.csmonitor.com/Business/Tax-VOX/2011/1021/ Tax-reform-is-essential-inevitable-and-impossible. Copyright © 2011 by Len Burman. All rights reserved. Reproduced by permission.

As you read, consider the following questions:

1. To what did the Tax Reform Act of 1986 cut the top individual tax rate, according to Burman?

2. Why was Dan Rostenkowski jailed, according to the viewpoint?

3. Why does Burman say that revenue-neutral tax reform was possible in 1986?

Twenty-five years ago tomorrow (October 21, 2011) [President] Ronald Reagan signed the Tax Reform Act of 1986 [TRA86]. It was a beautiful fall day and the signing was on the back lawn of the White House. I was there along with many of the other Treasury staff who worked on the historic legislation, as well as a busload of tourists from Iowa who were hoping for a White House tour, but had to settle for parts as extras in the stagecraft of official Washington. Because I am really tall (6'6"), one tourist asked me to take a picture of the scene, which she couldn't see through the crowd. I hope it came out.

I loved tax reform. It lured me away from the sleepy New England college where I was a professor and changed my life. Whether you judge TRA86 a success or a failure, it was a major change to the tax code. It cut top individual income tax rates from 50 to 28% and corporate rates from 46 to 34%. It eliminated a host of loopholes, deductions, and preferences— mostly on the corporate side. It removed poor people from the income tax rolls. It taxed capital gains the same as ordinary income, eliminating the single-biggest driver of individual income tax shelters and making it possible to slash top tax rates while maintaining the progressivity of the income tax.

Putting Together the Tax Reform Act of 1986

And it was fun. Treasury and Hill staff who worked on tax reform worked incredibly long hours crafting and re-crafting provisions as the bill evolved through its many permutations. It was thrilling. Even though almost nobody actually thought it would become law, imagining a complete rewrite of the tax code is about as much fun as a tax geek can have. We were rewriting the Internal Revenue Code of 1954. Exciting!

But there was little reason for optimism until late in the process. The first version that passed the House wasn't much of a reform. Compared with the pristine blueprint that Treasury produced for the president in 1984, the House bill had restored most of the loopholes and didn't cut rates much. The congressional leadership didn't look promising. [Committee on] Ways and Means chairman Dan Rostenkowski was an old-school Chicago pol [politician]. (Later, he'd go to jail for mail fraud.) Senate [Committee on] Finance chairman Bob Packwood used to have weekly meetings with his big donors where they'd tell him about their desires—none of which involved paring loopholes and deductions. (Packwood eventually retired in disgrace after several female staffers recounted his improper advances.) But at some point, these sleazy pols decided that reform was good politics. Ronald Reagan's style of benign neglect turned out to be perfect for tax reform. He'd be AWOL [absent without leave] for months, and then show up at a key point to make a great speech or do some arm-twisting. A junior senator from New Jersey, known more for his jump shot than his legislative prowess, turned out to be a master tactician and strategist. Bill Bradley, who later proved to be a lousy politician on the national stage when he ran for president, had unsurpassed skills in the back rooms and antechambers of Congress.

Somehow, after multiple near-death experiences, the Tax Reform Act passed with overwhelming bipartisan majorities in both Houses of Congress and was signed by the president on that beautiful fall day. I stayed in Washington, made some amazing friends, got to work on Health Reform I at CBO [Congressional Budget Office] in 1994, returned to the Treasury to head up the office where I'd been a staffer during tax reform, started the Tax Policy Center, and eventually returned to academia to hold a chair in memory of one of my legislative heroes, Pat Moynihan (who was a senior Democrat on Senate [Committee on] Finance during tax reform). I'm pretty sure none of that would have happened without tax reform, as I'd never have come to Washington in the first place. So I have just warm feelings about the Tax Reform Act of 1986.

Need for Reform Has Increased but Bipartisan Cooperation Has Eroded

And it's easy to get excited about the possibility of a Tax Reform Act of 2014. Tax reform is even more necessary now than it was in 1986. Everyone agrees that the tax system is complex, unfair, and inefficient. And it doesn't come close to raising enough revenue to pay for the government, whose needs will only grow as the baby boomers retire and health care costs continue to rise. There are lots of tax reform plans out there, including the ones produced by the Bipartisan Policy Center (my favorite since I helped write it), the Bowles-Simpson panel [referring to the National Commission on Fiscal Responsibility and Reform], and an excellent report commissioned by President [George W.] Bush. There's even an action-forcing event in 2012 when the Bush tax cuts are scheduled to expire. Rather than extending what everyone agrees is a deeply dysfunctional tax code, why not remake it to meet the needs of 21st-century America?

Cue the patriotic music.

The only problem is that tax reform is really, really hard and the political process in Washington has eroded far more than the tax code since 1986. Look at the keys to success in 1986. It was bipartisan—a real collaboration, not just two Republicans from New England or two Democrats from the South crossing party lines. In 1986, Republicans and Democrats disagreed as passionately about policy as they do now, but they didn't hate each other. They could see the possibility of major bipartisan legislation as a win-win. Now politics is a football game—a zero-sum game where either your team wins or the other team does. Win-win is not possible. (That's why the parties can continue finger-pointing while inaction keeps millions of Americans unemployed.)

There was presidential leadership. President Reagan, exalted now as the saint of Republican orthodoxy by his party, was astonishingly ideologically flexible in 1986. His only marching orders were to cut tax rates and keep some kind of tax subsidy for homeownership. Everything else was negotiable. He twisted arms in his own party and worked with Democrats in Congress to make compromise possible.

Could that happen now? President [Barack] Obama is probably no more ideological than President Reagan, but he has the problem that the Republicans in Congress hate him. Maybe if he wins a second term, and preventing his reelection is no longer the GOP priority, collaboration might be possible. But, more likely, the Republicans will be focused on winning seats in the midterm election of 2014 and setting the stage for a White House takeover in 2016. In this era of endless electioneering and political polarization, a bipartisan tax reform bill just seems a wistful dream.

Options for Revenue-Neutral Reform Have Disappeared

Then there's the question of what bipartisan tax reform might look like. The 1986 bill was revenue-neutral [not lowering or increasing revenue] and many in Congress are saying that's what we should do again. There are two problems with that. First, we need revenue. And, second, revenue-neutral tax reform happened in 1986 only because there was a giant honeypot available to sweeten the medicine. TRA86 used a giant corporate tax increase to pay for those big rate cuts for individuals. Since real people don't think that corporations are people (sorry, Mitt Romney), they were perfectly happy for companies to pay more so individuals would pay less. Most importantly, even corporate CEOs [chief executive officers] thought this was a good idea. A key point in the 1986 drama was when CEOs came to Washington to lobby for tax reform.

This time around, there are no giant corporate loopholes to close. A corporate tax increase is not in the cards. Revenue-neutral individual income tax reform would inevitably produce many millions of losers, and they'd object strenuously. I just don't think revenue-neutral reform is politically feasible. And, besides, we need more revenue.

In a more enlightened time, tax reform to help tame the deficit would make a lot of sense. Closing tax expenditures creates the possibility of cutting rates *and* raising revenue, which could improve economic efficiency (by deterring tax avoidance) and help forestall a debt catastrophe. But almost all the Republicans in Congress have vowed to never support such an option.

My bottom line: Tax reform has never been more necessary, it's hard to see a solution to our budget problems without it, and it's just impossible.

Periodical and Internet Sources Bibliography

The following articles have been selected to supplement the diverse views presented in this chapter.

Mike Alberti	"A New Deficit Narrative?," *Remapping Debate*, April 6, 2011.
Jamelle Bouie	"You Can Have Tax Cuts or Deficit Reduction but Not Both," *American Prospect*, June 6, 2011.
Jonathan Cohn	"Yes, Taxing the Rich Will Make a Difference," *New Republic*, July 27, 2011.
Adam Davidson	"It's Not Just About the Millionaires," *New York Times Magazine*, November 9, 2011.
Stephen F. Hayes	"Obama vs. Obama," *Weekly Standard*, July 11, 2011.
Art Levine	"Labor Pushing Backbone Implant for Wavering Dems on Taxes, Social Security, Deficits," *In These Times*, November 19, 2010.
David S. Logan	"The Proper Role of Taxes in Deficit and Debt Reduction," Tax Foundation, July 29, 2011. http://taxfoundation.org.
Jeanne Sahadi	"National Debt: Why Tax Revenue Has to Go Up," CNNMoney, September 6, 2011. http://money.cnn.com.
Thomas Sowell	"You Can't Tax the Rich," *National Review Online*, September 15, 2011. www.nationalreview.com.
Roberton Williams	"Will Obama's Budget Raise or Lower Taxes? Both," *Christian Science Monitor*, March 22, 2012.
Fareed Zakaria	"Raise My Taxes, Mr. President!," *Newsweek*, August 1, 2010.

OPPOSING
VIEWPOINTS®
SERIES

CHAPTER 3

Will Cuts to Entitlement Programs Reduce the Deficit?

Chapter Preface

As plans to deal with the US deficit are debated, one of the parts of the federal budget under scrutiny for proposed cuts is Social Security. Reaction to this proposal has been heated, eliciting some demands that the program be left intact and calls for massive cuts.

Once believed to be a program that could not be touched without incurring the wrath of the American voter, Social Security has repeatedly been analyzed for potential reductions as new plans for deficit reduction have emerged since 2010.

Social Security was enacted in 1935, when the United States was experiencing the Great Depression. At that time, about half of the people sixty-five and older were employed by others and one-sixth counted on public charity. Many had lost their savings in the economic collapse. Social Security was created to make sure that in the future the elderly would have enough income in retirement that they would not have to rely on welfare. Four years after the program started, coverage was extended to dependents and survivors.

Social Security was designed to provide post-retirement benefits based on workers' contributions into the system throughout their years of employment. Workers pay a 6.2 percent Social Security tax on their first $106,800 in wages, which is matched by employers. But the amount of benefits paid out by Social Security exceeded the amount that it collected in 2010—the first time that had happened since 1983. In 2011 Social Security paid $727 billion in benefits to more than fifty-five million people, representing about 20 percent of the federal budget and about 5 percent of the nation's total economic output, known as gross domestic product (GDP).

Nine out of ten Americans over age sixty-five collect Social Security benefits, which make up 41 percent of the income, on average. Sixty-nine percent of Social Security total benefits are paid to retired workers and their dependents, and 19 percent of total benefits are paid to disabled workers and their dependents. In 2012 alone, $760 billion in Social Security benefits were paid to more than fifty-six million Americans. With such large expenditures and portions of the population at stake, organizations on both sides of the issue are fighting to protect their interests.

The Campaign for America's Future held an October 2011 conference called "Take Back the American Dream" to show its opposition to changes in Social Security. The organization hopes to spur a grassroots movement like the one in 2005 that defeated President George W. Bush's drive to privatize Social Security. The organization's view is that Social Security should not be dismissed as an entitlement program. At a gathering during the conference, a member of the crowd shouted, "Call them earned benefits, not entitlements. We worked for them." Even those groups that have long lobbied for no reductions or changes to Social Security such as AARP, an advocacy group for Americans age fifty and older, are now acknowledging that change is inevitable and are working behind the scenes to make sure the results of the changes arc as favorable as possible.

Other groups think it is time for Social Security to be done away with entirely. These groups believe the federal government never had the authority under the Constitution to offer such a retirement program to America's elderly. Some support privatization, a plan in which retirement funds would no longer be guaranteed in a fund held by the federal government but instead would be invested in the stock market by individuals. Others propose that the states take on responsibility for Social Security.

What role reforms or cuts to Social Security could play in lowering the US deficit is one of the issues examined in the following chapter of *Opposing Viewpoints: The US Deficit*. Other topics explored are whether it is necessary to cut Medicare, how health care costs play into decisions regarding the future of Social Security and Medicare, and what impact the aging US population has on entitlements spending and attempts to balance the budget.

> *"You are not going to get to a balanced budget by cutting domestic discretionary spending. . . . You could eliminate it all, and we would still face a budget deficit this year of more than $680 billion."*

Cuts to Entitlements and Other Programs Are Essential to Reduce the Deficit

Michael Tanner

Michael Tanner is a senior fellow at the Cato Institute and author of Leviathan on the Right: How Big-Government Conservatism Brought Down the Republican Revolution. *In the following viewpoint, he argues that even though voters do not support cuts to entitlement programs—Social Security and Medicare—they do want spending reduced and are against increasing the deficit. The only spending targets that most taxpayers agree should be cut, such as foreign aid, make up far too little of the budget to make a difference in the deficit, Tanner asserts. Large programs such as defense, he adds, must be cut, and expensive entitlement programs must be reformed to solve the country's*

Michael Tanner, "This Is Going to Hurt: There Is No Painless Way to Balance the Budget," *National Review*, April 6, 2011. http://www.nationalreview.com/articles/263972/going-hurt-michael-tanner. Copyright © 2011 by the National Review. All rights reserved. Reproduced by permission.

budget problems. Tanner also maintains that raising taxes on the wealthy is only a short-term boost to the economy and not a long-term solution to revenue shortfalls or deficit reduction.

As you read, consider the following questions:

1. According to a Reuters/Ipsos poll cited in the viewpoint, what percentage of Americans oppose raising the debt ceiling?

2. What percentage of federal spending is accounted for by defense, according to Tanner?

3. According to the viewpoint, what percentage of voters are opposed to cutting Medicare?

Want to know just how bad our budget problems are? The 2012 budget plan unveiled yesterday (April 5, 2011) by Rep. Paul Ryan and Republican House leaders cuts federal spending by $6.2 trillion over the next ten years—and still adds $6 trillion to the national debt.

Yet, by and large, Americans still believe there is a painless way to balance the budget. They have a better chance searching for that pot of gold at the end of the rainbow.

That's not to say that Americans don't understand the need to balance our budget. Most Americans want spending cut and the budget balanced. In fact, a recent Reuters/Ipsos poll showed that fully 71 percent of voters oppose raising the current $14.3 trillion debt ceiling.

But when it comes to what to cut, voters have a hard time finding anything they are willing to go without. Of course, everyone is against "fraud, waste, and abuse." And certainly there is a great deal of that in the federal budget. But there is no line item called "fraud, waste, and abuse." One can't go in and simply slice waste off the top of the budget. Rather, it is marbled throughout in ways that often defy easy cutting. Moreover, one person's boondoggle [government-funded pro-

Americans Are Resistant to Economically Necessary Entitlements and Subsidy Cuts

60% of voters indicated that maintaining entitlement programs at current levels was more important than reducing federal deficits. And many U.S. households and businesses receiving tax subsidies and other government benefits strongly resist having them reduced—even in order to lower deficits.

Tony Downs, "Downs Issues Warning: Cut Entitlements or Risk Further Economic Deterioration," National Real Estate Investor, *August 2, 2011.*

gram funded as a political favor that is not helpful or useful to society] is another person's critical program.

And when it comes to programs, there are remarkably few that the public seems willing to cut. For example, we've increased federal education spending by 188 percent in real terms since 1975 without any improvement in outcomes. Yet just 24 percent of voters say they support cuts in federal education spending. A majority of Americans also oppose cutting antipoverty programs, homeland security, aid to farmers, and funding for the arts and sciences.

Small Programs Are Popular Targets for Budget Cuts

Indeed, about the only program the public seems anxious to cut is foreign aid—not surprising, since voters think it consumes 10 percent of federal spending. The actual figure is slightly less than 1 percent. The public also wants to cut the benefits and pensions of government workers. They believe that makes up another 10 percent of the budget. In reality, it is 3.5 percent. That's not an argument against cutting foreign aid or the excessive benefits of government workers, but you aren't going to get to a balanced budget that way.

In fact, you are not going to get to a balanced budget by cutting domestic discretionary spending. All domestic discretionary spending, everything from the FBI [Federal Bureau of Investigation] to the FDA [Food and Drug Administration], from the Department of Commerce to the Department of Education, makes up just 18 percent of the federal budget. You could eliminate it all, and we would still face a budget deficit this year of more than $680 billion.

And while we are at it, 57 percent of voters oppose cuts in defense spending. Defense, of course, accounts for another 19 percent of federal spending. It will have to be on the table if the budget is ever going to be balanced.

In the end, the only real way to bring the federal budget into long-term balance is to reform entitlement programs, as Ryan has proposed doing. But here again, the public is reluctant to support cuts. According to the most recent Gallup poll, two-thirds of Americans oppose cutting Social Security benefits. Even self-professed supporters of the Tea Party oppose cutting Social Security by 2–1. Nearly as many voters, 61 percent, oppose cutting Medicare.

On the other side of the ledger, Americans are slightly more willing to raise taxes to balance the budget—but only on the "rich," usually defined as someone earning a lot more than they do. But, of course, taxing the rich won't get you to a balanced budget either. Even setting aside the damage to the economy that tax increases would do, you simply can't get enough money out of the rich to solve our fiscal problems. In fact, if you confiscated—not just taxed, but confiscated—all the wealth of every millionaire in America, you could come close to covering our current national debt. But once entitlements start to really kick in, in about a decade or so, we'd be in trouble again.

Steep Tax Hikes Are Counterproductive

Any tax increase that would make a dent in our long-term debt would have to go well beyond the rich, biting deeply into the middle class. But tax hikes of that magnitude would devastate economic growth and prove counterproductive in the end. Simply put, we can't tax our way out of this hole.

So if you want to know why we are in trouble, look no further than us. If we are serious about avoiding the fiscal train wreck to come, we are going to have to be willing to cut even those programs we like. There can be no sacred cows. Everything has to be on the table.

Ryan's approach is a good start. But for the long term, it will require a 2012 presidential candidate capable of explaining the facts to an uninformed public and courageous enough to make the necessary cuts—even if the public thinks they hurt.

> *"Cutting spending when the economy is weak is bad policy and bad economics. Struggling economies must grow their way out of recession by spending liberally and putting people back to work, thus adding to government revenues."*

Cuts to Crucial Government Programs Will Make the Deficit Larger

Mike Whitney

Mike Whitney writes about politics and economics from a libertarian perspective. In the following viewpoint, he argues that the federal government should continue to stimulate the economy by spending enough to support it until American wages and consumer power increase and the debt load decreases. Without increased government spending to help Americans find work, reduce their debt, and renegotiate mortgages, Whitney maintains, the economy can never fully recover and return to sustained growth, because consumption and consumers drive growth. Whitney cites numerous examples to support the benefits of increasing spending to stimulate recovery and declares that what little recovery has taken place is due to the economic stimulus plan

Mike Whitney, "Cutting Government Spending Will Increase the Budget Deficit," *The Market Oracle*, August 31, 2011. http://www.marketoracle.co.uk/Article30209.html. Copyright © 2011 by Mike Whitney. All rights reserved. Reproduced by permission.

implemented by the Barack Obama administration. In addition to increasing spending on programs to support individual Americans, he concludes, the US government must support the labor market to correct inequities that are evidenced by the fact that corporations continue to profit while workers suffer.

As you read, consider the following questions:

1. What is the current percentage of US household debt as a share of annual disposable income, according to Whitney?

2. How much equity did US households extract from their homes using home equity loans from 2003 to the third quarter of 2008, according to the viewpoint?

3. How much does Kelly Evans, cited in the viewpoint, report that US corporate profits have jumped since the recession ended in 2009?

The US consumer's decade-long spending spree has ended, but there's still an ocean of red ink left to mop up. And with housing prices falling and unemployment tipping 9 percent, it will take longer to clear the family balance sheet than many had anticipated.

Traditionally, the government has helped to ease the pain of deleveraging [reducing debt by selling assets] by providing fiscal stimulus to boost economic activity and lower the real cost of debt. But Capitol Hill is now in the grips of deficit hawks who frown on such Keynesian [based on the theories of macroeconomics established by famous economist John Maynard Keynes] remedies, so households and consumers will have to fend for themselves and pay down debts as best they can or default when repayment is no longer possible. That's bad news for the economy that depends on consumers for 71 percent of GDP [gross domestic product]. Without a healthy consumer, the economy will face years of sluggishness and stagnation.

U.S. household debt as a share of annual disposable income is currently 115 percent, down from the peak of 135 percent in 2008. But, while consumers are making headway in paring down their debts, there's still a lot of work to do. Economists believe that the figure will eventually return to its historic range of 75 percent, which means slower growth for years to come unless someone else makes up the difference in spending.

But what sector is big enough to make up for the loss in consumer spending? Business? Government?

American Wages and Purchasing Power Need to Recover

Business spending is still significantly below pre-crisis levels of investment. Naturally, businesses aren't going to hire more workers and produce more products if demand is weak. And, demand is bound to stay weak if there's no rebound in consumption. But how can the consumer rebound when he's buried under a mountain of debt and making every effort to increase his savings? Surely, if wages were growing, then it would be easier to pay down debts while increasing spending at the same time. But wages aren't growing, in fact, they are falling in inflation-adjusted terms. So personal consumption—which typically leads the way out of recession—will continue to disappoint. This is from an article by Stephen [S.] Roach titled "One Number Says It All":

> There are two distinct phases to this period of unprecedented US consumer weakness. From the first quarter of 2008 through the second period of 2009, consumer demand fell for six consecutive quarters at a 2.2% annual rate. Not surprisingly, the contraction was most acute during the depths of the Great Crisis, when consumption plunged at a 4.5% rate in the third and fourth quarters of 2008.

> As the US economy bottomed out in mid-2009, consumers entered a second phase—a very subdued recovery. Annual-

ized real consumption growth over the subsequent eight-quarter period from the third quarter of 2009 through the second quarter of 2011 averaged 2.1%. That is the most anemic consumer recovery on record—fully 1.5 percentage points slower than the 12-year pre-crisis trend of 3.6% that prevailed between 1996 and 2007.

These figures are a good deal weaker than originally stated. As part of the annual reworking of the US national income and product accounts that was released in July 2011, Commerce Department statisticians slashed their earlier estimates of consumer spending. The 14-quarter growth trend from early 2008 to mid-2011 was cut from 0.5% to 0.2%; the bulk of the downward revision was concentrated in the first six quarters of this period—for which the estimate of the annualized consumption decline was doubled, from 1.1% to 2.2%.

I have been tracking these so-called benchmark revisions for about 40 years. This is, by far, one of the most significant I have ever seen. We all knew it was tough for the American consumer—but this revision portrays the crisis-induced cutbacks and subsequent anemic recovery in a much dimmer light. ("One Number Says It All," Stephen S. Roach, Project Syndicate)

There Can Be No Economic Recovery Without Stimulus

Roach's time line is key to understanding what's going on. He says: "the subsequent eight-quarter period from the third quarter of 2009 through the second quarter of 2011 averaged 2.1%." The period that Roach calls a "very subdued recovery" coincides with the implementation of the $787 billion fiscal stimulus (ARRA [American Recovery and Reinvestment Act]). Absent the [President Barack] Obama administration's fiscal intervention, there would have been no recovery. This is worth considering in view of the fact that households continue to pay down debts and will do so for the foreseeable future. If the government doesn't provide additional stimulus, then the economy will slip back into negative territory. And that's precisely what's happening now. Here's an excerpt from an article by John P. Hussman, PhD, Hussman Funds, who connects the dots drawing from recent data:

> It is now urgent for investors to recognize that the set of economic evidence we observe reflects a unique signature of recessions comprising deterioration in financial and economic measures that is always and only observed during or immediately prior to U.S. recessions. These include a widening of credit spreads on corporate debt versus 6 months prior, the S&P 500 [Standard & Poor's 500, financial rating index] below its level of 6 months prior, the Treasury yield curve flatter than 2.5% . . . , year-over-year GDP growth below 2%, ISM [Institute for Supply Management] Purchasing Managers Index below 54, year-over-year growth in total nonfarm payrolls below 1%, as well as important corroborating indicators such as plunging consumer confidence. There are certainly a great number of opinions about the prospect of recession, but the evidence we observe at present has 100% sensitivity (these conditions have always been observed during or just prior to each U.S. recession) and 100% specificity (the only time we observe the full set of these conditions is during or just prior to U.S. recessions). This doesn't mean that the U.S. economy cannot possibly avoid a recession, but to expect that outcome relies on the hope that "this time is different." ("A Reprieve from Misguided Recklessness," John P. Hussman, PhD, Hussman Funds)

Policy should be based on more than hope. It should be grounded in a firm grasp of macroeconomics and a commitment to the common good.

Peak Growth Coincided with Peak Spending

Keep in mind, that during the peak bubble years of 2000 to 2007 households nearly doubled their "outstanding debt to

Using Government Spending and Taxation to Stimulate Economic Growth

Fiscal policy is an important tool for managing the economy because of its ability to affect the total amount of output produced—that is, gross domestic product. The first impact of a fiscal expansion is to raise the demand for goods and services. This greater demand leads to increases in both output and prices. The degree to which higher demand increases output and prices depends, in turn, on the state of the business cycle. If the economy is in recession, with unused productive capacity and unemployed workers, then increases in demand will lead mostly to more output without changing the price level. If the economy is at full employment, by contrast, a fiscal expansion will have more effect on prices and less impact on total output.

David N. Weil, "Fiscal Policy,"
The Concise Encyclopedia of Economics,
Library of Economics and Liberty, 2008.

$13.8 trillion" and "personal consumption grew by 44% from $6.9 trillion to $9.9 trillion." Also, from 2003 to the third quarter 2008, US households extracted $2.3 trillion of equity from their homes in the form of home equity loans and cash-out refinancings." (Figures from "Will US Consumer Debt Reduction Cripple the Recovery?," McKinsey Global Institute)

$2.3 trillion! Think about that. That's nearly $500 billion that was being pumped into the economy every year, which is more than Obama's $787 stimulus distributed over a two-year period. That's why unemployment stayed low while housing prices ballooned, because loose lending standards and easy money inflated the biggest credit bubble of all time. But now the trend has reversed itself and debt-deflation dynamics are in play forcing consumers to cut spending, increase saving, and pay down their debts. Only the federal government has the ability and the wherewithal to support the flagging economy while the process continues. The government must boost its spending, increase the deficits, and assist in the deleveraging process. This is from an article by economist Laura [D'Andrea] Tyson titled "Recovering from a Balance-Sheet Recession":

> In other recoveries during the last 50 years, public sector employment increased. This time it is falling: During the last year, the private sector added 1.8 million jobs while the public sector cut 550,000.
>
> What should policy makers do to combat the large and lingering job losses that result from a financial crisis and balance-sheet recession? Mr. [Richard] Koo, whose book on Japan's experience should be required reading for members of Congress, showed that when the private sector is curtailing spending, fiscal stimulus to increase growth and reduce unemployment is the most effective way to reduce the private sector debt overhang choking private spending.
>
> When the Japanese government tried fiscal consolidation to slow the growth of government debt in response to International Monetary Fund advice in 1997, the results were economic contraction and an increase in the government deficit. In contrast, when the Japanese government increased government spending, the pace of recovery strengthened and the deficit as a share of gross domestic product declined. ("Recovering from a Balance-Sheet Recession," Laura D'Andrea Tyson, *New York Times*)

The Japanese Experience Demonstrates the Dangers of Cutting Spending

Did you catch that? When the Japanese government tried to decrease the deficits by slashing spending, they increased the deficits. This is the lesson that every country in the EU [European Union]—which has applied the ECB-IMF [European Central Bank–International Monetary Fund] austerity measures—has learned. Cutting spending when the economy is weak is bad policy and bad economics. Struggling economies must grow their way out of recession by spending liberally and putting people back to work, thus adding to government revenues. Here's Tyson again explaining why this is so:

> The market understands that the most important driver of the fiscal deficit in the short to medium run is weak tax revenues, reflecting slow growth and high unemployment, and that additional fiscal measures to put people back to work are the most effective way to reduce the deficit.
>
> Every one percentage point of growth adds about $2.5 trillion in government revenue. An extra percentage point of growth over the next five years would do more to reduce the deficit during that period than any of the spending cuts currently under discussion. And faster growth would make it easier for the private sector to reduce its debt burden. . . . Under these conditions, slow growth leads to a higher debt ratio, not vice versa. . . . ("Recovering from a Balance-Sheet Recession," Laura D'Andrea Tyson, *New York Times*)

So, how do we speed up the deleveraging process so the economy can get back on track?

First, the government must be committed to long-term "sustained" fiscal stimulus until the share of household debt to disposable income returns to normal. Second, there should be a restructuring of household and personal debts "including"—as economist Carmen Reinhart says—"debt forgiveness for low-income Americans."

"Until we deal head-on with the fact that some of those debts are not ever going to be repaid, we will continue to have this shadow over growth," Reinhart told Bloomberg news last weekend [in August 2011].

Debt repudiation, principle write-downs on underwater mortgages and amnesty on delinquent student loans should all be added to the mix of stimulants to future growth.

Government Must Support Jobs and the Labor Market

Finally—along with federally funded government jobs programs (a revised WPA [Works Progress Administration], etc.)—Congress needs to address the chronic supply-demand imbalance that has emerged from labor's dwindling share in corporate profits. The imbalance has now reached historic levels which has widened gross inequality and threatens to keep the economy in a semipermanent state of depression. Here's a quick summary from Barry Ritholtz's *The Big Picture* [blog]:

> Labor share averaged 64.3 percent from 1947 to 2000. Labor share has declined over the past decade, falling to its lowest point in the third quarter of 2010, 57.8 percent. The change in labor share from one period to the next has become a major factor contributing to the compensation-productivity gap in the nonfarm business sector....
>
> While labor share has recently plummeted to all-time lows since record keeping began, median household income has stagnated for the past 12 years. In the last recession (2001), incomes had only begun to decline.... One decade later, labor share has collapsed, incomes have gone nowhere, and credit availability . . . has all but vanished except for the most creditworthy." ("The Heart of the Matter," *The Big Picture*)

Not only is labor getting a smaller and smaller piece of the pie, but also financial engineering—spurred on by low interest rates and deregulation—has given rise to consecutive credit bubbles which have transferred a larger share of pension and retirement-fund wealth to Wall Street speculators. So, working people are not just getting screwed on their labor, the government and central bank are actually helping to facilitate the pilfering of their savings.

Corporate Profits Illustrate Economic Imbalance

At the same time, corporate profits have continued to skyrocket. As the *Wall Street Journal*'s Kelly Evans notes, "Since the recession ended in mid-2009, U.S. corporate profits have jumped by about 43% to a record $1.45 trillion as of the first quarter, after taxes, inventory and accounting adjustments, according to the Commerce Department." ("More Liquidity Only Douses Growth Sparks," *Wall Street Journal*)

So, despite sky-high unemployment, household deleveraging, historic inequality and slow growth, profits keep rising. Is there any doubt about whose interests are being served?

The only way out of the mess that workers find themselves in is through politics. And—on that score—FDR [Franklin Delano Roosevelt] said it best: "We cannot allow our economic life to be controlled by that small group of men whose chief outlook upon the social welfare is tinctured by the fact that they can make huge profits from the lending of money and the marketing of securities—an outlook which deserves the adjectives 'selfish' and 'opportunist.'" (Franklin Delano Roosevelt, "FDR Explains the Crisis: Why It Feels Like 1932," Pam Martens, *CounterPunch*)

> *"Done right, Medicare-for-All would significantly reverse the U.S. economic crisis."*

Medicare Reforms Benefiting Middle and Lower Income Americans Could Reduce the Deficit

Michele Swenson

Michele Swenson is a former nurse and author of Democracy Under Assault: TheoPolitics, Incivility and Violence on the Right. *In the following viewpoint, she maintains that a national health program will contain the health care costs that are a large contributor to the national budget deficit. Swenson characterizes the debate over health care in Congress as far too focused upon deficit reduction at the expense of programs like Medicare and Medicaid. If Democrats would make the case that health care reform was the key to economic recovery, she asserts, support for a single-payer health care program, which she refers to as "Medicare-for-All," could be achieved. She concludes that wealthy corporate interests are being served at the expense of working Americans under current health care policies and that to correct this inequity and promote full economic recovery the Democrats must support a single-payer health care program.*

Michele Swenson, "Medicare: 'Biggest Deficit Driver' or 'Solution' to Economic Recovery?," *Daily Kos*, May 26, 2011. Reproduced by permission.

As you read, consider the following questions:

1. What does Dr. Ron Forthofer propose for military expenditures, according to the viewpoint?

2. How much in cuts to Medicare does the Bowles-Simpson plan call for, according to Swenson?

3. How could Medicare-for-All save $58–400 billion annually, according to the viewpoint?

Political actors in Washington and corporate media often bounce off each other as though in an echo chamber. So it was no surprise to hear NPR's [National Public Radio's] national political correspondent Mara Liasson refer to Medicare as the "biggest driver" of the deficit. Never mind that health care in general, at 1/6 of the economy, is the biggest economic cost driver—a problem that health care reformers failed to address. Controlling the rise of premium and administrative health costs would significantly bend Medicare and Medicaid costs, as would paying for quality instead of quantity care, and permitting negotiation of bulk drug rates.

Health care is one of many concessions by Democrats in the deficit debate. Perhaps their biggest concession to Republicans is that "entitlements"—Medicare, Medicaid and Social Security—have to be cut. "Entitlement" as used by the political right implies payments to the un-deserving: Rep. Paul Ryan cautioned that the safety net should "not become a hammock that lulls able-bodied citizens into lives of complacency and dependency." "Entitlement" more aptly describes the presumption of rightful due of big rewards to Wall St. crooks who are paid handsomely for the practice of bundling derivatives and speculation at the expense of mortgage holders.

Ryan's budget proposal [of 2011] belies the pretense of reducing the debt, except on the backs of seniors and the poor,

> ## Medicare Is a Solution
>
> Medicare isn't the problem. It's the solution.
>
> The real problem is the soaring costs of health care that lie beneath Medicare. They're costs all of us are bearing in the form of soaring premiums, co-payments, and deductibles.
>
> *Robert Reich, "Mr. President: Why Medicare Isn't the Problem, It's the Solution," RobertReich.org, April 12, 2011. http://robertreich.org.*

as he proposes reducing the top income tax rate to just 25 percent, even as corporate profits soar, wages flatline and unemployment remains intractable.

Dr. Ron Forthofer of Colorado, a retired professor of biostatistics, writes that the deficit commission report is narrowly focused, placing sacrifice on the backs of working people. Obviously, it is easier to go after grandma and teachers than "the entrenched financial/corporate power structure." Among Dr. Forthofer's alternative proposals for savings: 1) Eliminate at least $200 billion of annual corporate welfare; 2) Reduce military expenditures by 50 percent over five years; 3) Eliminate the rampant fraud and waste in military contracting; 4) Reverse the wasteful privatization of many military and other public jobs; 5) End the counterproductive occupations of Afghanistan and Iraq; 6) Place fees on all speculative trades/activities; 7) Restore [President Dwight D.] Eisenhower-era tax levels; and 8) Enact Medicare for all instead of the [Patient Protection and] Affordable Care Act [passed in 2010 and providing expanded coverage and restrictions on insurance carriers so they cannot reject applicants based on preexisting conditions] that does nothing to control health care costs.

Negotiations Are Heavily Weighted Toward Cutting Medicare

Democrats have handicapped themselves by starting with compromise in talks regarding the economy and deficit reduction, just as they did with health care reform. Negotiations over Medicare-for-deficit-reduction shake down to Republican Ryan's plan to eliminate the program, privatizing it with vouchers on the one hand, and Democrats' agreement to baseline Medicare cuts on the other. The 3 Democrats and 3 Republicans in the "Gang of Six" tasked with deficit reduction, have started with the baseline of the Bowles-Simpson deficit reduction plan [referring to the recommendations of the National Commission on Fiscal Responsibility and Reform that is chaired by Erskine Bowles and Alan K. Simpson], which calls for $400 billion in Medicare cuts over a decade (on top of $500 billion in cuts called for in the [Patient Protection and] Affordable Care Act, achieved mostly by ending Medicare Advantage overpayments).

Sen. Tom Coburn (R-OK) dropped out of the "Gang of Six" after demanding and failing to get "immediate and deep cuts" to current Medicare beneficiaries—an additional $130 billion (totaling $530 billion).

What Simpson and Bowles term "increased cost sharing . . . to promote informed consumer health choices and spending" amounts to a greater shift of Medicare costs to seniors. The commission's proposed cuts include elimination of "first-dollar coverage in Medigap [insurance coverage purchased to cover expenses not paid for by Medicare] plans" and establishment of "a universal deductible, a single coinsurance rate, and a catastrophic coverage cap in Medicare." In short, seniors will pay a lot more out of pocket, as Medicare is turned into Republicans' pretense of "free market" access, their idealized vision of elimination of social insurance: Health care will be available only to those who can afford to pay outright.

By failing to make the best case for health care reform as essential to economic recovery, Democrats have relinquished to Republicans the narrative surrounding the economy and health care.

Much of Democratic self-talk is self-defeating. On a telephone town hall meeting with Rep. Diana DeGette (D-CO) last week [in May 2011], the first question was asked by a nurse who had lived in Great Britain for a period of time. *Health care is easily accessible and cost-effective in Great Britain, so why don't we have something similar here?* Rep. DeGette's quick reply was "There are not the votes in Congress for single payer [single payer refers to an insurance system in which one company or government entity pays for benefits]"—another case of Democrats' folding to self-fulfilling prophesy before the case is made. Republicans relentlessly hammer a position until they achieve their goal. Democrats concede the debate before it begins. The case for Medicare-for-All was never made, in fact was avoided, preceding passage of the [Patient Protection and] Affordable Care Act. The insurance and Big Pharma [referring to the pharmaceutical industry] had the president's ear, not the majority of people who favored at the very least a "public option."

Whatever his leadership style, President [Barack] Obama has failed to use the bully pulpit where it counts most—on economic and health care reform. He caved on extending [President George W.] Bush tax cuts at a time when a large majority opposed them. At the same time, he jeopardized the future of Social Security by agreeing to Social Security payroll tax cuts. Subsequently, the president was portrayed on *Saturday Night Live* totally submissive to his Republican hostage takers, suffering from Stockholm Syndrome [the psychological tendency of a hostage to sympathize with his captor]. Cartoonist Mike Luckovich illustrated "Obama Poker Tips"— showing his cards and cheerfully giving the shirt off his back.

Medicare-for-All Is the Best Way to Cut Health Care Costs and the Deficit

Meanwhile, Republican efforts to eliminate/gut health care in general, and Medicare specifically, exacerbates the deficit about which all profess concern. Republican-designed Medicare Part D is highly inflationary and contributes greatly to the deficit. It denies negotiation of bulk drug rates, while granting billions in taxpayer-funded insurance subsidies for programs like private Medicare Advantage, which costs 11% more than traditional Medicare, with no added services. Negotiation of bulk drug rates could have been, but was not, added as a feature of the [Patient Protection and] Affordable Care Act.

Done right, Medicare-for-All would significantly reverse the U.S. economic crisis. Former labor secretary Robert Reich writes, "Medicare isn't the problem. It's the solution" to economic recovery.

- By expanding the risk pool to include both the healthy young and the sick elderly, Medicare-for-All would save $58–400 billion annually, much of the savings from streamlined administrative costs.

- More Americans would get quality health care, and Medicare-for-All would significantly ease our economic crisis and sharply reduce the long-term budget crisis.

- Medicare and Medicaid should be permitted to use their bargaining power to negotiate lower rates with hospitals, doctors and pharmaceutical companies.

- Reforming payment to reward quality care, not quantity, will also save.

If Democrats are to reclaim the role of leadership, they must define issues in terms of a moral imperative to create true economic justice and recovery for the benefit of working people, instead of capitulating to corporate power and serving the economic bottom line of the wealthy elite.

> "When people say we have to drastically overhaul Medicare, they generally don't provide the numbers to back up that claim. That's because they can't."

Cutting Medicare Spending Is Unnecessary Because It Is an Affordable Program

James Kwak

James Kwak is an associate professor at the University of Connecticut School of Law, and he is coauthor of White House Burning: The Founding Fathers, Our National Debt, and Why It Matters to You. *In the following viewpoint, he argues that only minor fixes are needed to keep Medicare affordable. Kwak asserts that the so-called "crisis" of Medicare spending has been manufactured to further the interests of those who wish to profit from substituting private insurance for government-run health care. These private insurance plans, Kwak declares, would actually cost more than Medicare, for individual Americans and for the country at large. Further, he declares, Medicare was never designed to be an entirely self-funding program; rather, he says, it was supposed to run a deficit, and it does. However, he notes,*

James Kwak, "Hey, Washington: We Don't Have to Overhaul Medicare to Save It," *Atlantic*, December 20, 2011. http://www.theatlantic.com/business/archive/2011/12/hey-washington-we-dont-have-to-overhaul-medicare-to-save-it/250282. Copyright © by the Atlantic. All rights reserved. Reproduced by permission.

this deficit is just 1 percent of gross domestic product. To pay for this program, he maintains, the United States could increase revenue from taxes by ending the tax exemption for employer-provided health benefits and by raising the Medicare payroll tax.

As you read, consider the following questions:

1. How many people does Kwak say are uninsured?

2. How much does Kwak say the payroll tax for Medicare has been increased since 1986?

3. What percentage of GDP will government health care spending be in 2040, according to the viewpoint?

Medicare needs a structural overhaul in order to avoid bankrupting the federal government—or so Republicans and many Democrats would have you believe. The latest evidence of this consensus is the [2011] Paul Ryan-Ron Wyden proposal to change Medicare into a voucher system where traditional Medicare is one of the options, but there are artificial caps on the value of the vouchers.

There's only one problem with this consensus. It's wrong.

The push for Medicare reform comes from understandable concerns about health care. Rising medical costs are a serious problem. We spend more than people in other countries, we get less, our gains in life expectancy are mediocre, employers are struggling with increasing health care costs, and of course, 50 million people are uninsured.

Second, rising health care costs are the most important factor in the federal government's long-term deficit. The CBO [Congressional Budget Office] projects that spending on Medicare, Medicaid, CHIP [Children's Health Insurance Program], and subsidies for insurance purchased through exchanges will grow from 5.4 percent of GDP [gross domestic product] this year to 10.3 percent in 2035, and that's assuming a slight slowdown in the growth rate of health care spending. . . .

Third, policies that actually reduce the overall, economy-wide price level for health care—for example, by shifting toward payment methods that focus on outcomes and promote accountability—are good. We should do all of that that we can.

There Is No Medicare Crisis

But policies that simply shift costs from the federal government onto families—like arbitrary caps on the growth rate of "Medicare" vouchers—are worse than pointless. Substituting out-of-pocket spending for government spending doesn't save the American people any money. In fact, it is likely to only increase costs, since Medicare has more purchasing power than private health care plans. Policies like Ryan-Wyden only make sense if they can reduce the overall price level—but there's no evidence that competition in the private insurance market can reduce health care costs. There is, however, evidence that it will only increase costs. . . .

When people say we have to drastically overhaul Medicare, they generally don't provide the numbers to back up that claim. That's because they can't. Let's take a look.

First of all, we have to know how much money Medicare loses today. It's important to realize that Medicare was never designed to be self-funding. Part A (hospital insurance) was supposed to be self-funding through payroll taxes, but Parts B and C were always meant to draw on general government revenues in addition to beneficiary premiums. In 2010, Part A's deficit was $48 billion, or 0.3% of GDP. . . . Parts B and C together ran a deficit of $205 billion (funding from general revenue, which by construction fills the gap between expenses and other income), or 1.4% of GDP, for a total deficit of 1.7% of GDP.

Then we have to know how much worse that deficit is going to get. (Remember, Medicare was always supposed to run a deficit.) By 2040, Part A's deficit will double as a percentage

"Do away with all the tax loopholes you want, but don't mess with my entitlements," cartoon by Harley Schwadron, www.CartoonStock.com. Copyright © by Harley Schwadron. Reproduction rights obtainable from www.CartoonStock.com. Reproduced by permission.

of taxable payroll, so it should be about 0.7% of GDP. The Part B/C deficit will be 2.3% of GDP, for a total of 3.0% of GDP.

In other words, over the next three decades, Medicare's additional contribution to annual deficits will only be 1.3% of GDP.

We Can Afford Medicare

That's not peanuts, but there are plenty of ways to pay for it. For one thing, we could eliminate the tax exclusion for employer health plans, which currently costs the Treasury Department 1.9% of GDP, including lost income taxes and lost payroll taxes. Forty percent of the value of this exclusion currently goes to households in the top income quintile. If we eliminate the tax exclusion and use half of the proceeds to fund rebates to low-income households, we save 0.9% of GDP right there. Increase the Medicare payroll tax by 1 percentage point (from a level that hasn't changed since 1986, despite twenty-five years of rising health care costs) and you get another 0.5% of GDP. In other words, those two policy changes alone—one of which eliminates a distorting subsidy that largely goes to the well off—could buy us 30 years of Medicare.

You may say that this is only sticking fingers in the dike, since health care costs will continue to grow. But this ignores another important fact: Revenues are growing, too, not only in real terms but as a share of the economy. A major reason for this is what's called "real bracket creep." Even though the tax brackets are indexed, they are only indexed to inflation. Over time, as real incomes rise, more and more incomes slide into the higher tax brackets. Most people think that people who make more money can and should pay higher taxes; by that logic, it's perfectly fair that people pay higher taxes as they make more money over time.

So, for example, the CBO says that most government health care spending will grow from 6.9% of GDP in 2020 to 11.4% in 2040, which looks scary. But it also says that, under current law, tax revenues will grow from 20.6% of GDP to 24.2% over the same time period—which means that four-fifths of the growth in health care spending is covered by growth in tax revenues. (If the [George W.] Bush tax cuts are extended, the 2020 starting point for revenues will be lower, but the growth rate of tax revenues will be similar.)

In summary, if you look closely, the deterioration of Medicare's finances (1.3 percentage points over three decades) is not as big as most people would have you believe. And if someone tells you about rising long-term health care spending under current law, he should also tell you that tax revenues are rising in the long term under current law.

The people who say Medicare has to be radically trans-formed, though, just don't know the numbers. Or they do, but they ignore them either because they hate social insurance or because they want to raid Medicare spending to fund tax cuts for the rich.

You may think traditional Medicare is a bad program. It does have its problems. Most notably, it's based on the fee-for-service model that produces high costs and poor care. But if you want to get rid of it, you should argue that it's a flawed program instead of hiding behind the myth that we can't af-ford it.

| *"Whether for its own sake or for the country's fiscal viability, Social Security must be reformed; and the sooner we act, the better."*

Social Security Spending Is a Major Contributor to the Deficit and Must Be Cut

Committee for a Responsible Federal Budget

The Committee for a Responsible Federal Budget is a bipartisan, nonprofit organization committed to educating the public about issues that have significant fiscal policy impact. In the following viewpoint, the committee argues that it is critical to begin to reform Social Security sooner rather than later. Whether Social Security is viewed as a self-funding program that adds nothing to the deficit, or as a giant government program that leads to deficits because it spends more than it takes in, the committee asserts, the program's funds will soon run out. If it is not reformed, drastic cuts in benefits will have to be instituted. Rather than allowing this to happen, the committee suggests, it is advisable to implement gradual changes to taxes and benefits so that the program can be sustained without creating a crisis situation for beneficiaries or for the budget.

"Social Security and the Budget," Committee for a Responsible Federal Budget, New America Foundation, March 24, 2011. http://crfb.org/document/social-security-and-budget. Copyright © 2011 by Committee for a Responsible Federal Budget. All rights reserved. Reproduced by permission.

As you read, consider the following questions:

1. What percentage of the economy is consumed by Social Security, according to the viewpoint?

2. By what year do the authors say that Social Security's trust fund will run out of money?

3. How much will Social Security's negative cash balance add to the deficit from 2011 through 2021, according to the viewpoint?

There has been a good deal of discussion recently over Social Security's effect on the federal budget. Some argue that Social Security is an independent and self-financing program which does not add a dime to the deficit, while others suggest that it is the largest government program and—because it spends more than it raises—contributes to overall budget deficits.

In reality, both perspectives are correct, depending on how you view the program. It is legitimate to consider Social Security either as an independent (off-budget) and self-financed program or as part of the overall (unified) federal budget.

From the first perspective, Social Security can finance its costs for another 25 years through a combination of dedicated revenue and trust fund assets. True, the trust funds are invested in government bonds—but since Social Security essentially lent to the rest of the government over the past two decades, it is entitled to collect on those loans.

From the second perspective, Social Security is already adding to the deficit today since benefits exceed dedicated revenues, and will do so by increasing amounts in the coming years. Currently, the program consumes about 20 percent of the budget and 4.8 percent of the economy. But its costs will grow to over 6.1 percent of the economy over the next quarter century, while its dedicated revenues will actually fall somewhat. This gulf will substantially add to the budget deficit and debt.

Either of these frameworks is sensible. Ironically, though, both frameworks should lead policy makers to the same conclusion: whether for its own sake or for the country's fiscal viability, Social Security must be reformed; and the sooner we act, the better.

Social Security Viewed as an Independent Program

The first way to view Social Security is as an independent program, financed from its own trust funds and dedicated revenues.

Because Social Security has been collecting more in revenues than it has been paying in benefits over the last two decades, the trust funds have built up substantial reserves. Today, it holds about $2.6 trillion in special issue government bonds, the equivalent of about 3.5 years' worth of benefits. Though the system is now collecting a little bit less in revenue than it pays out, the existence of these bonds (and the interest they generate) will allow Social Security to pay full benefits for the next quarter century.

Social Security nonetheless faces a serious solvency problem. The trust funds have already begun to fall relative to annual benefits, and will decline in nominal terms by 2025 or earlier. By 2037, the trust funds will run out of money and the program will only be able to pay benefits based on revenue received—meaning an across-the-board and immediate 22 percent cut in benefits for all beneficiaries, including those who will have already retired.

Avoiding this for the next 75 years would require closing an actuarial gap of 0.7 percent of GDP (1.92 percent of payroll). Making the program sustainably solvent—so that it does not fall out of solvency outside the 75-year budget window—would require also closing the vast majority of the 1.4 percent of GDP (4.12 percent of payroll) cash-flow deficits in the 75th year.

A Brief History of Social Security

During the height of the Great Depression and at the urging of President Franklin D. Roosevelt, Congress created Social Security to protect the elderly from the worst ravages of poverty. Roosevelt's vision was as simple as it was profound: All the elderly must be protected from the ravages of poverty and ensured enough income for a reasonable standard of living. Due to political opposition to welfare programs and increases in the budget, however, Roosevelt sold the program as a retirement investment program that would not add to the federal budget. . . . This has led to perpetual confusion, since although the Social Security program does not add to the budget, it is not a pension fund at all but an income transfer program from one generation to another.

David Hilfiker,
"Common Sense on Social Security,"
DavidHilfiker.com, November 15, 2010.

Social Security as a Share of the Federal Budget

An alternative way to view Social Security is as part of the overall budget. Currently, one out of every five dollars the government spends goes to Social Security—and a similar amount of the government's financing (revenues plus borrowing) comes from the Social Security payroll tax and the taxation of Social Security benefits.

Under this approach, the Social Security program is already contributing to the deficit today. Any time the program's costs exceed its revenues, it must withdraw from either the interest from or the principle of its trust funds. Yet these trust funds are invested completely in government bonds and thus must be repaid from general revenues, or the rest of the budget.

Putting aside the issue of whether or not past surpluses have been "saved" in an economic sense, it is important to recognize that the government must produce the cash to repay the trust fund assets. Absent other tax or spending changes, this will mean going on the open market to borrow the funds.

Social Security's negative cash balance will become an increasing burden to the rest of government, *adding nearly $600 billion to the deficit from 2011 through 2021 alone*. As population aging causes the program's costs to grow as a share of the economy (and revenues to shrink somewhat as workers retire), the net effect of the program will be to increase the unified budget deficit by 0.4 percent of GDP in 2020 and 1.3 percent in 2035 (excluding interest). Failure to close this gap will mean either permanently higher budget deficits, or else will require other tax provisions and spending programs to be modified more significantly in order to subsidize Social Security. . . .

Under the latest projections—which CBO [Congressional Budget Office] has released since the 2010 Social Security Trustees report—Social Security is now projected to be in permanent deficit. These deficits will grow over time, adding trillions of dollars to future deficits.

Policy Changes Are Needed Soon

Regardless of how you view the program, the sooner we make policy changes to the program, the better.

Viewed as its own separate program, the need for Social Security reform is quite compelling. Social Security is on a road toward insolvency and is projected to run out of money by 2037—at which point current law calls for a 22 percent across-the-board benefit cut. Making the system solvent for the next 75 years will require making changes equal to 0.7

percent of GDP (1.92 percent of payroll). It will also require getting the program into eventual cash balance (or close to it) to make sure solvency is *sustainable* and will not be undermined by a one-year change of the valuation period.

The longer we wait to enact changes, the larger those adjustments will need to be to make the system solvent. For example, the current actuarial shortfall through 2085 is roughly 0.7 percent of GDP. Waiting ten years would increase the size of the shortfall (through 2085) to 0.9 percent of GDP, and waiting until 2037 would increase it to 1.3 percent. In other words, the longer we wait, the larger the necessary adjustment to achieve solvency through 2085.

For those who regard Social Security as part of the budget, putting the program into cash-flow balance is important and would help alleviate pressure on the rest of the budget. Not only is it the single largest government program, and thus an important part of any meaningful budget fix, its costs will increase by 1.3 percent of GDP by 2035 (it has already grown by 0.7 percent of GDP since 2000).

Unfortunately, getting to immediate cash-flow balance would be extraordinarily difficult given current demographic pressures and the political problems associated with significantly cutting benefits for current retires. However, making gradual changes starting now can lead to significant savings over time and put the program back on a path toward cash-flow balance.

No matter how you look at it, Social Security is in dire need of reform. The program's trustees continue to warn us that changes need to be implemented as soon as possible. By acting now, we can implement changes in thoughtful ways and protect those who depend on the program the most. We can also institute tax and benefit changes gradually, giving current workers plenty of time to adjust their retirement planning decisions.

Whether for the health of the budget or for its own sake, it's time to reform Social Security.

"The [balanced budget] amendment's mandate would negatively impact Social Security by diminishing the safeguards of the trust fund surpluses and burdening future generations."

Social Security Does Not Add to the Deficit and Cuts Could Destroy the Program

National Committee to Preserve Social Security and Medicare

The National Committee to Preserve Social Security and Medicare is a nonprofit, nonpartisan organization that works toward developing a secure retirement for all Americans. In the following viewpoint, the committee outlines its opposition to a balanced budget amendment to the US Constitution. Such an amendment, the committee argues, would destroy the whole premise behind Social Security and other entitlement programs—namely, that they are paid for in advance by working people and held in trust for them. The amendment would unnecessarily burden lower income Americans who depend on social programs, the committee asserts, and would impose unrealistic and danger-

"A Constitutional Balanced Budget Amendment Threatens Social Security," Government Relations and Policy, July 2011. http://www.ncpssm.org/news/archive/vp_constitutional_balanced_budget/. Copyright © 2011 by the National Committee to Preserve Social Security & Medicare. All rights reserved. Reproduced by permission.

ous limits on spending that would threaten the government's ability to fund essential activities as well as its ability to help its citizens in emergencies or times of economic hardship.

As you read, consider the following questions:

1. When will Social Security surpluses peak at $3.7 trillion, according to the viewpoint?

2. How much per year do the authors say people with incomes over $1 million would receive in tax reductions if the Bush tax cuts are made permanent?

3. According to the viewpoint, what percentage of GDP were federal expenditures during the Ronald Reagan administration?

The House Committee on the Judiciary recently [July 2011] reported out H.J. Res. 1, a proposal to write a balanced budget amendment into the Constitution. H.J. Res. 1 would require a balanced budget every year regardless of the state of the economy, unless a supermajority of both houses overrode that requirement. Unlike past versions of a balance budget amendment, H.J. Res. 1 would also impose an arbitrary and unrealistic spending cap of 18 percent of gross domestic product (GDP), a level not seen since 1965. The government would be allowed to exceed this cap only if approved by two-thirds of the full Congress. The proposed amendment would also limit any increase to the debt ceiling unless approved by three-fifths of the whole number of the House and Senate, and prohibit any increases in revenue unless agreed to by two-thirds of Congress.

As a result, this version of the balanced budget amendment would require draconian spending cuts of such a magnitude as to force policy makers to severely slash Medicare, Medicaid, and many other programs while opening the door to massive new tax cuts. At the same time, it would make it very difficult to achieve balance through revenue raisers such as tax increases or to raise the debt ceiling. Furthermore, the amendment's mandate would negatively impact Social Security by diminishing the safeguards of the trust fund surpluses and burdening future generations.

A Balanced Budget Amendment Would Negatively Impact Social Security

The balanced budget amendment's mandate that total government expenditures in any year cannot exceed total revenues collected in the same year poses far-reaching implications for Social Security. This would mean the budget would be considered balanced when the deficit outside Social Security exactly offsets the surplus inside Social Security. Therefore, the objective of accumulating a Social Security surplus to help the nation to pay for future retiree benefits would be stymied. Moreover, the benefits of current retirees would likely have to be financed in full by the taxes of those currently working.

The 1983 bipartisan Social Security commission moved Social Security from a pure "pay-as-you-go" system to one under which the baby boomers would contribute more toward their own retirement. As a result, Social Security has built up sizable surpluses that will peak in 2022 at $3.7 trillion. The balanced budget amendment, however, would undermine this approach to protecting Social Security and promoting generational equity. Under a balanced budget amendment, total government expenditures in any year—including expenditures for Social Security benefits—could not exceed total revenues collected in the same year, including revenues from Social Security payroll taxes.

Therefore, even though the Social Security trust funds have accumulated large balances, drawing down any part of those balances would mean the trust funds were spending more in benefits in those years than they were receiving in taxes. That would result in impermissible deficit spending. Such deficit spending could be offset by a corresponding surplus in the rest of the budget; however, achieving a sizable surplus in the rest of the budget would be a daunting and almost unachievable task, especially given the sharp increase in Medicare and Medicaid costs. The requirement that the constitutional amendment would impose in this area is akin to requiring a family to pay for a child's college tuition for a given year entirely out of that same year's earnings, rather than allowing the family to save money for this purpose in prior years or to borrow money for college that is paid back after the child graduates.

A Balanced Budget Amendment Would Favor Wealthy over Middle and Lower Income Americans

While the balanced budget amendment does not dictate any particular approach to deficit reduction, by altering established congressional voting procedures it increases the likelihood that the fiscal policies adopted in coming decades will favor the well off at the expense of middle- and low-income Americans. The amendment would require a two-thirds vote of the full membership of the House and Senate to raise taxes. Spending cuts, by contrast, would continue to require only a majority of those present and voting, and could be passed on a voice vote.

Not only would this essentially rule out any revenue contribution to deficit reduction, it also would mean that once a new tax cut opened up, it would become virtually impossible to close. Wealthy individuals and large corporations receive most of their government benefits through tax subsidies. By contrast, low- and middle-income families receive most of their benefits through government programs. A constitutional amendment that makes it harder to reduce tax subsidies than to cut programs tends to favor the affluent over Americans of lesser means.

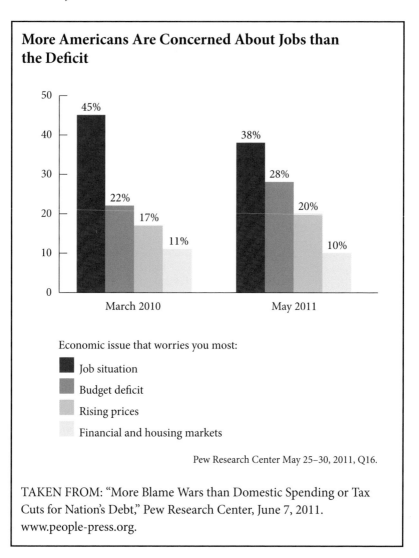

More Americans Are Concerned About Jobs than the Deficit

Economic issue that worries you most:

- Job situation
- Budget deficit
- Rising prices
- Financial and housing markets

Pew Research Center May 25–30, 2011, Q16.

TAKEN FROM: "More Blame Wars than Domestic Spending or Tax Cuts for Nation's Debt," Pew Research Center, June 7, 2011. www.people-press.org.

Furthermore, this balanced budget amendment would pave the way for significant new tax cuts. Because this amendment would cap federal spending at 18 percent of GDP, revenues could be reduced to that level as well. Most sponsors of the amendment favor making permanent all of President [George W.] Bush's tax cuts of 2001 and 2003, including those for the wealthiest Americans. Those tax cuts give people with incomes of more than $1 million tax reductions that average more than $125,000 a year.

A Balanced Budget Amendment Would Threaten Federal Economic Stability

H.J. Res. 1 would limit annual federal spending to 18 percent of GDP. By writing an arbitrary and unrealistic cap on federal spending into the Constitution, H.J. Res. 1 would force draconian cuts in programs like Medicare and Social Security. The last time federal spending averaged 18 percent of GDP was in 1965. Coincidentally, that was the same year that the Medicaid and Medicare programs were established. Even during President Ronald Regan's administration, federal expenditures averaged 22 percent of GDP. Moreover, that spending level occurred at a time when no members of the baby boom generation had yet retired and total health care spending was one-third lower a share of GDP than today. Even if spending and revenues were in balance, a spending cap would limit the government's ability to address the needs of its citizens or respond to economic downturns and emergencies.

Adding to these problems, the amendment would heighten the risk of a federal government default by requiring three-fifths vote of both the House and the Senate to raise the debt limit. Currently, only a simple majority is required to raise the debt ceiling, yet Congress has still found it increasingly difficult to secure the votes needed.

Consider the scenario where budgets thought to be balanced at the start of a fiscal year fall out of balance during the year as a result of factors such as slower-than-expected economic growth or natural disasters. If sizable deficits emerged with only part of the year remaining, Congress and the president may be unable to agree on a package of budget cuts needed to restore balance in the remaining months of the year. As a result, Congress may be unable to amass three-fifths majorities in both chambers to raise the debt limit and allow a deficit. The president may be bound, at the point at which the "government runs out of money," to stop issuing checks.

"The truth is that we have a huge problem of exploding health care costs, part
of which shows up in Medicare and
Medicaid spending."

Cuts Should Be Made to Health Care Costs, Not to Entitlement Programs

Alan S. Blinder

Alan S. Blinder is a professor of economics and public affairs at Princeton University and a former vice chairman of the Federal Reserve. In the following viewpoint, he argues that although most Americans want to lower the US deficit, they have radically different opinions on how to do that, and it is not one of their top priorities. Blinder says that the United States can still attract investors to fund government programs with loans that can be paid off gradually, in the future; he adds that the focus on deficit reduction is too shortsighted to deal with a long-term deficit problem. He concludes that the biggest driver of the deficit is the cost of health care; without that cost, he insists, the budget would be within the target range as a percentage of gross domestic product.

Alan S. Blinder, "Four Deficit Myths and a Frightening Fact," *Wall Street Journal*, January 19, 2012. http://online.wsj.com/article/SB10001424052970204468004577164820504397092.html. Copyright © 2012 by Alan Blinder. All rights reserved. Reproduced by permission.

As you read, consider the following questions:

1. What is the one government expenditure that Blinder says Americans are willing to cut?

2. What does the CBO project the deficit will be as a percentage of GDP by 2040, according to Blinder?

3. What accounts for all of the projected rise in primary deficit by 2050, according to the viewpoint?

Try to ignore the current shallowness in American politics, if you can, and assume that the federal budget deficit will be among the major issues of the 2012 campaign. It certainly should be, for while everyone wants a lower deficit, the two parties have starkly different visions of how to get there.

Sadly, however, the public debate over the deficit is full of misconceptions and falsehoods. Remember the Moynihan principle? The late senator from New York [Patrick Moynihan] once said that everyone is entitled to his own opinion, but not to his own facts. In that spirit, I'd like to explode four myths now masquerading as facts.

Myth No. 1 is that the American people now demand deficit reduction as never before. Don't believe it. Yes, if you ask Americans about the deficit, they'll tell you they hate it—as they always have. But opinion polls show that the budget deficit is nowhere close to being Economic Public Enemy No 1. People care far more about high unemployment, the weak economy and the like.

Furthermore, once the discussion gets down to specifics, it is difficult to find anything the public favors that would make a serious dent in the deficit. No higher taxes, please, except on millionaires. No cuts in big programs like Social Security or Medicare.

Maybe defense cuts; attitudes about that vary from time to time. The one thing Americans consistently want to cut is foreign aid, which constitutes a minuscule share of U.S. government spending. Thus the attraction to lower deficits is only skin deep. It has always been thus. Poll numbers on these matters today look much the same as they did 20 or 30 years ago.

Investors Want to Lend the United States Money

Myth No. 2 is that America's deficit problem is so acute that government spending must be cut right now, despite the struggling economy. And any fiscal stimulus, even the payroll-tax extension, must be "paid for" immediately.

Wrong. Strange as it may seem with trillion-dollar-plus deficits, the U.S. government doesn't have a short-run borrowing problem at all. On the contrary, investors all over the world are clamoring to lend us money at negative real interest rates. In purchasing power terms, they are paying the U.S. government to borrow their money!

We should accept more of these gracious offers and use the funds to finance pressing needs for jobs programs, infrastructure projects, even mortgage foreclosure mitigation. And because the U.S. really does have a humongous long-run deficit problem, we can and should commit now to paying for any such spending many times over—but later. For example, it would be smart to borrow, say, another $500 billion this year and then pay for it, say, 10 times over, with $5 trillion in deficit reduction spread over 10 years—starting, say, in 2014.

Myth No. 3 [is that] for several years now, our political system has focused exclusively on the 10-year cumulative budget deficit. Whether it's proposals like 2010's Bowles-Simpson [referring to the National Commission on Fiscal Responsibility and Reform chaired by Erskine Bowles and Alan K. Simpson] or Domenici-Rivlin [referring to the Debt Reduction Task Force chaired by Pete Domenici and Alice Rivlin], the ill-fated Obama-Boehner "grand bargain" [referring to recommendations by President Barack Obama and Congressman

John Boehner on legislation to cut entitlements and raise new revenue], or the failure of the so-called Super Committee [the Joint Select Committee on Deficit Reduction], every high-profile deficit-reduction plan has focused on the next 10 years. In truth, however, what happens over the next decade barely matters. Our deficit problem—and it is a whopper—is much longer term than that.

According to the most recent long-run projections from the Congressional Budget Office [CBO], the federal deficit as a share of gross domestic product will shrink from its current bloated level for several years even without further action. The real deficit problem comes in the 2020s, 2030s and beyond. And it is huge. The CBO projections show the deficit bottoming out at 5.6% of GDP in 2014, rising to an astonishing 12.7% of GDP by 2030, to an unthinkable 18.4% of GDP by 2040, and continuing to rise further after that.

What drives this projected deficit explosion? . . .

Health Care Costs Are the Biggest Driver of Increased Deficits

Myth No. 4 is that America has a generalized problem of runaway spending, one that requires cuts across the board. No. The truth is that we have a huge problem of exploding health care costs, part of which shows up in Medicare and Medicaid spending.

Economists focus on the primary deficit, which includes everything except interest payments, on the grounds that the interest bill on the national debt is a consequence of past decisions. Policy initiatives can't change the government's interest payments. But they can reduce the primary deficit, now or in the future, by either spending less or taxing more.

According to the CBO, if nothing is done, the primary deficit will bottom out at 2.6% of GDP in 2018 and then rise to 7.4% of GDP by 2040. Where will the additional 4.8% of GDP come from? Remarkably, every penny will come from health care spending, which balloons from 6.6% of GDP to 11.4% in the projections, or 4.8% more of GDP. This exact match is just a coincidence, of course. If we use 2050 as the end point instead of 2040, the projected primary deficit increases by 6% of GDP, of which health care spending accounts for 6.6 percentage points. Yes, you read that right: Apart from increased health care costs, the rest of the primary deficit actually falls relative to GDP.

The CBO projects federal spending on all purposes other than health care and interest to be roughly stable as a share of GDP from 2015 to 2035, and then to drift lower. So no, America, we don't have a generalized overspending problem for the long run. We have a humongous health care problem.

If we could replace the Four Myths by the Four Facts, that would transform the nature of the public debate, focusing attention on what matters rather than what does not. But alas, this is an election year, creating an environment in which facts don't flourish. As we Brooklyn Dodgers fans used to say: Wait 'til next year.

| *"Population aging will remain a bigger financial challenge even than health cost inflation for decades to come."*

Entitlement Spending Must Be Cut Because the US Population Is Aging

Charles Blahous

Charles Blahous, a Hoover Institution research fellow, currently serves as one of the two public trustees for the Social Security and Medicare programs. In the following viewpoint, he puts forward his response to what he characterizes as erroneous beliefs about entitlement programs that he says are causing damaging policy decisions when it comes to the deficit. Blahous argues that it is the aging US population, specifically the baby boom generation, that is the greatest contributor to entitlement program overruns rather than other factors often cited, such as health care costs. He adds that Social Security represents as much of a threat to US financial instability as Medicare or Medicaid, and that the funding shortfalls in the programs are far greater than commentators are admitting. He concludes that because Social Security benefits for previous generations are paid for by those currently working, if there are more beneficiaries than workers, future generations will have to pay more to receive the same benefits.

Charles Blahous, "Five Myths About Social Security and Medicare," *Hoover Institution Journal*, August 26 2011. http://www.hoover.org/publications/defining-ideas/article/90721. Copyright © 2011 by Charles Blahous. All rights reserved. Reproduced by permission.

As you read, consider the following questions:

1. By what year is the vast majority of long-term cost growth in Social Security and Medicare expected to take place, according to the viewpoint?

2. How long does the author say is the most Social Security insolvency would be delayed in 90 percent of projections?

3. What percentage of their lifetime wage income will those entering the system lose to Social Security, according to the viewpoint?

The national discussion on entitlement programs is dazed and confused.

The federal government's largest two programs, Social Security and Medicare, are at the center of a vibrant national debate over our fiscal future. Each program faces a significant financial shortfall, the solution to which remains elusive.

The following are five myths that have been particularly damaging to our national discussion of Social Security and Medicare.

This elusiveness exists in part because of inherent substantive difficulties: Many Americans will have to give up something to bridge the significant gaps between program revenues and promised benefits. It's not easy to forge bipartisan agreement over how to allocate these sacrifices. Yet these decisions have been made unnecessarily difficult by rampant confusion about each program's finances.

The Aging US Population Presents a Greater Economic Threat than Health Care Inflation

MYTH #1: We "only" have a health care financing problem, not a population-aging or senior-entitlement problem. Medicare's financing shortfall is therefore much bigger and more urgent than Social Security's.

Unlike many myths that arise from popular ignorance, this damaging myth gained currency through being pushed by several influential policy advocates.

Make no mistake: The growth of health care costs is indeed a huge problem. But mainstream budget analysts have long understood that the graying of the baby boom generation would by itself create enormous financial challenges. When the boomers left the ranks of taxpaying workers and entered the ranks of Social Security and Medicare beneficiaries, federal expenditures would soar. These financial strains would be great enough to require a reassessment both of the annual benefits promised to these birth cohorts, and of the number of years they should be allowed to spend in subsidized retirement.

But as George W. Bush's second term drew toward a close, many of Washington's influential policy wonks began to sing a different tune. Suddenly population aging wasn't such a big deal. Even Social Security itself didn't face such a large problem. The entire fiscal shortfall was due, it was now said, to health care alone.

Proponents of this new line of argument were legion. Brookings Institution scholar Henry Aaron asserted flatly that "there is no general entitlement problem. Rather, the nation faces a daunting health care financing problem. . . ." AARP head Bill Novelli echoed the new line, saying that "we don't have an age problem; we have a health care cost problem." When Peter Orszag (Novelli's cited source for his claim) became director of the Congressional Budget Office (CBO), that agency soon published a controversial chart purporting to show that health care inflation utterly dwarfed population aging as a contributor to the long-term fiscal imbalance. CBO corrected this in later publications, but a lasting misimpression had already been made.

This line was enormously attractive to politicians then assuming office at both ends of Pennsylvania Avenue. President

Barack Obama himself soon declared, "Make no mistake, health care reform is entitlement reform." If Social Security specifically and population aging generally were minor problems, politicians were off the hook for tough calls concerning benefit levels and eligibility ages. Expert opinion was now offering a rationale for doing what politicians liked best—*expanding* promised benefits—instead of warning of the necessity of scaling untenable promises *back*. One direct consequence of this widely repeated rhetoric was the passage of yet another federal health entitlement last year.

Population Aging, More than Health Care Inflation, Drives Entitlement Spending

All of this inflicted incalculable damage upon prospects for righting federal finances, as deficit hawks knew all along that it would. While the urgency of Social Security reform was downplayed, its finances deteriorated even more rapidly than previously projected. The troublesome long-term budget outlook that some had attributed entirely to unreformed health care now remains just as bleak after health care reform. Indeed, the health legislation erected still more barriers to fiscal consolidation, for example, when the Obama administration declared that the new law's insurance exchanges were to remain untouched in recent budget negotiations.

Even if it hadn't been so damaging, the myth would still be flatly untrue. While Medicare as a *whole* poses the larger financial challenge over the long term, Social Security's shortfall is of comparable magnitude and is by some actuarial measures even larger. The latest trustees' reports find that Social Security's imbalance equals 2.22 percent of its tax base over the next 75 years ($6.5 trillion in present value), whereas Medicare's is 0.79 percent ($3.0 trillion). And from now through 2025, Social Security will not only remain the more expensive of the two programs, it will actually grow more in the aggregate.

In sum, population aging will remain a bigger financial challenge even than health cost inflation for decades to come. The vast majority of long-term cost growth in Social Security and Medicare, for example, is projected to take place by 2035. The CBO now attributes 64 percent of cost growth through 2035 in Social Security, Medicare, *and* Medicaid to population aging, even though two of these programs are health entitlements.

There is of course a kernel of truth in the myth—just enough to permit its wide circulation. *If* we could muddle through to 2035 without altering our spending commitments, and *if* excess health cost inflation persisted as the health sector swallowed larger fractions of the nation's economy, then indeed we would later reach a point where health care costs overwhelmed all other federal budgetary problems. But no such hypothetical excuses the irresponsible implication that we could indefinitely defer revising our entitlement benefit promises to seniors.

This myth has inspired terrible policy mistakes and cost us valuable time in confronting the most pressing financial problems we face. For Social Security *does* face a huge financial challenge—indeed, quite comparable to Medicare's—and population aging still remains the most problematic driver of unsustainable federal spending growth.

MYTH #2: Social Security does not and cannot add to the deficit.

In 2011, Social Security tax income will fall short of payment obligations and the program will add $151 billion to the current federal deficit. Despite this, vocal opponents of Social Security reform have commanded the attention of the press and key public figures when asserting that the program does not add to the deficit. In deference to this rhetorical pressure, elected officials ranging from the Senate's "Gang of Six" [referring to three Democratic and three Republican senators tasked with deficit reduction] to the president have insisted that Social Security reform take place entirely separately from deficit reduction talks.

Social Security Adds to the Deficit

Some historical background is important to understanding why this is fiction. From 1984–2009 inclusive, Social Security did indeed mitigate federal deficits by running annual surpluses of taxes over expenditures. But that positive balance turned into a deficit in 2010 when the onset of baby boomer retirements coincided with a recession that depressed payroll tax revenues. Social Security is thus now exacerbating the federal budget deficit and will do so even more in the years ahead.

The argument that Social Security "can't add to the deficit" is founded on the idea that the program is self-financing, so it can't spend on benefits beyond what it previously generated in revenues. The money and spending authority now in Social Security's trust funds, it is asserted, simply represent the amount by which the program has thus far *reduced* federal deficits. In 2036, therefore, when the trust funds are depleted, the program's net effect on the debt to date would theoretically be zero. It can never become a net negative, so the story goes, because the program lacks borrowing authority.

Much of this might well hold water were it not for certain unavoidable realities. First, not all of the money in Social Security's trust funds represents past surplus taxes paid by *anyone*. Some of the debt was simply issued without any incoming taxes behind it. This year [2011], for example, the Social Security payroll tax was cut while—to make up for the lost revenue—the same law issued $105 billion in further Treasury bonds to its trust funds.

Moreover, Social Security is only "not adding to the deficit" this year if we credit the program for interest payments and other transfers of general government revenues. But the

CBO is absolutely explicit that such payments do not mitigate the program's effect of adding to the deficit: "because those interest transactions represent payments from one part of the government (the general fund of the Treasury) to another (the Social Security trust funds), they do not affect federal budget deficits or surpluses."

Indeed, the vast majority of all assets in the trust funds represent such interest credits. These interest payments would only reflect a positive long-term budget impact if past surplus Social Security taxes had been saved. Most academic analysis has instead concluded the opposite—that past surpluses stimulated additional federal consumption—instead of being used to reduce federal debt service costs.

In sum, Social Security is clearly adding to the deficit this year—it will add far more in the years to come under current law.

Medicare's Hospital Insurance Trust Fund Is Not a Complete Indicator of the Program's Financial Condition

MYTH #3: Medicare's projected insolvency date is the critical barometer of its financial condition.

This year, the Medicare trustees (of which I am one) projected that the Medicare [health insurance] trust fund would be insolvent [unable to pay debts] in 2024, five years earlier than projected in the 2010 trustees' report. This five-year acceleration was depicted in press accounts as a serious deterioration of Medicare's finances.

Medicare's finances are indeed in dire condition and people are right to be concerned about them. Medicare's insolvency date, however, is at best an incomplete measure of the program's finances for at least four reasons.

First, it refers to just one portion of Medicare financing—the hospital insurance fund, or Part A. But Medicare also has a Part B and a Part D funded through another trust fund. Because these other parts (B and D) of Medicare are provided by law with the revenues required to match expected costs, solvency is not a meaningful concept for them. The one part of Medicare for which the 2024 insolvency date is relevant actually represents less than *half* of Medicare's total cost.

Second, because Medicare's trust fund balances are kept small, even minor annual changes in program finances can cause the projected depletion date to change by several years. The latest five-year deterioration didn't, for example, reflect a qualitative change. To the contrary, in no year prior to the insolvency date did the new report show an annual worsening (relative to the previous report) even as large as -0.25 percent of the program's tax base.

Third, trust fund solvency only signifies the extent of the program's financing *authority*; this is very different from the government's actual *ability* to finance benefits. In 2010, for example, the trustees' report found that Medicare provisions in the new health care law would extend [health insurance] solvency from 2017 to 2029. But other provisions in that same law spent the vast majority of those savings on a new health entitlement. Though this effect would undo much of the supposed improvement in the government's ability to pay, it is not captured in the trustees' projections.

Finally—as with Social Security—Medicare's insolvency date can be manipulated by government accounting. Congress can issue additional debt to Medicare's trust funds at any time, thereby extending its period of projected solvency without improving the government's ability to finance Medicare by so much as a penny.

Social Security's Financing Shortfall Is Very Real and Very Certain

MYTH #4: Social Security projections are conservative; a good portion of its projected shortfall might disappear on its own.

This myth has faded of late as Social Security's finances are now far worse than its trustees previously projected. But in recent years, it was almost an article of faith on the American left that the trustees had been exaggerating the Social Security shortfall with overly conservative projections. It can still be heard on occasion, as in Paul Krugman's recent statement that "there's a significant chance, according to [the program's actuaries'] estimates, that [trust fund exhaustion] will never come."

Actually, there isn't such a significant chance. A statistical analysis prepared by the Social Security actuaries [statisticians] for the trustees actually shows that in 90 percent of all projection scenarios, the most that program insolvency would be delayed would be only six years. Moreover, what Krugman refers to as a "significant chance" represents much less than a 1-in-50 probability.

The historical basis for this myth was a fundamental confusion about the elements of current forecasts. Some wrongly assumed that the trustees were projecting a slowdown in national productivity growth. What the trustees (like other credible forecasters) actually project is a slowing of net national labor force growth as the large baby boom generation retires. Aggregate economic growth is equal to the product of productivity growth times growth in the number of workers. Just as New York's economy grew more slowly than Texas's over the last decade because Texas's population grew faster, our national economy will grow more slowly if workforce growth slows. In fact, contrary to the myth, the trustees actually assume that real wage growth will somewhat *increase* going forward.

A number of commentators have even asserted that the trustees had a history of overly conservative projections, particularly with respect to economic growth. This was, as I stated in a paper presented at the American Enterprise Institute [for Public Policy Research] in 2007, "empirically incorrect," as the trustees had been "not a bit too conservative in predicting the present." And in the aftermath of the recent recession, Social Security is now experiencing deficits at an earlier date than predicted in *any* previous trustees' report since the 1983 reforms.

The argument that the trustees were being "too conservative" has turned out to be nearly 180 degrees from reality. But even before the recent recession, there was never a reasonable analytical basis for it.

"Pay-as-You-Go" Means Older Americans' Benefits Are Paid for by Younger Ones Who Will Lose Net Income in the Exchange

MYTH #5: Social Security's projected solvency through 2036 means that beneficiaries have prepaid their benefits through that date; any benefit changes, therefore, should be deferred until later.

This unfortunate myth leads to great confusion as to what constitutes a "fair" reform of Social Security.

Workers do not pay in advance for their own benefits under current Social Security law. Rather, the vast majority of each generation's Social Security payroll taxes are used to pay for the benefits of the *previous* generation of beneficiaries.

This method of financing, known as "pay-as-you-go," has clear implications for the intergenerational fairness (or unfairness) of Social Security. As the ratio of workers to beneficiaries declines, each succeeding generation must pay a higher tax rate to get the same relative benefit "replacement rate." In other words, pay-as-you-go financing treats younger generations worse and worse as society ages.

Some numbers from the trustees' report demonstrate the point. If current benefit schedules are left in place, those now entering the system will lose roughly 4 percent of their lifetime wage income to Social Security, *even if they in turn receive all benefits now scheduled for them.* Postponing financial corrections until the baby boomers are all in retirement thus does not result in workers getting "what they paid for," but rather results in the *least* equitable treatment across generations.

The reason that the trust fund is projected to last until 2036 is not because baby boomers have pre-funded a quarter century's worth of benefit payments. To the contrary, the trust funds are never projected to hold enough assets to fund more than about three-and-a-half years' worth of payments. From now through 2036, well more than four-fifths of the funds to finance benefit payments will be derived from taxes coming in from younger workers.

In sum, the suggestion that Social Security benefits have been "prepaid" through 2036 is incorrect and fosters substantial confusion about what constitutes an equitable solution to the program's financial shortfall.

These five myths are by no means the only myths that confuse our national discussions of Social Security and Medicare. They are, however, particularly damaging myths of which policy makers would do well to disabuse themselves.

Periodical and Internet Sources Bibliography

The following articles have been selected to supplement the diverse views presented in this chapter.

Massimo Calabresi	"The (Smart) Politics of Punting on Entitlements," *Time*, February 15, 2011.
Thomas Ferguson and Robert Johnson	"The Truth About the Deficit and Social Security," *Salon*, July 7, 2011. www.salon.com.
Jim Geraghty	"Balancing the Budget on the Backs of Metaphors," *National Review Online*, September 19, 2011. www.nationalreview.com.
James Kwak	"Moment of Blather," *The Baseline Scenario*, April 5, 2011. http://baselinescenario.com.
Sara Murray	"Budget Solution: Squeeze the Middle," *Wall Street Journal*, July 13, 2011.
Wendy Patton	"Don't Let Poor and Middle Class Bear Burden of Deficit Reduction," *Cleveland Plain Dealer*, November 19, 2011.
Robert Restuccia and Adam Searing	"How to Cut Health Care Costs Without Gutting Medicare," *Charlotte Observer*, October 30, 2011.
Julie Rovner	"Medicare Key to Conquering Deficit Dilemma," NPR, December 1, 2010. www.npr.org.
Robert J. Samuelson	"Social Security Is Welfare," *Washington Post*, March 7, 2011.
Ruy Teixeira	"Public Opinion Snapshot: Public Is Strongly Against Cutting Medicare," Center for American Progress, April 25, 2011. www.americanprogress.org.

OPPOSING
VIEWPOINTS®
SERIES

CHAPTER 4

Should Defense Spending Be Cut to Reduce the Deficit?

Chapter Preface

In 2001 Lockheed Martin won the largest Pentagon contract ever, the one to build the F-35 Lightning II. The fighter plane was to be the most cost-effective solution to military air-power needs. The key to this monetary savings was that the plane would be used by the US Air Force, Navy, and Marines. It would essentially be one plane modified to meet the needs of each of the respective branches of the armed services. The winning design employed the advanced stealth technology developed for the Air Force's F-22 fighter.

The initial development contract was for $19 billion and expected to grow to $200 billion over the life of the program, with the Pentagon ordering at least three thousand of the fighters. The British Royal Navy and Air Force and the Royal Norwegian Air Force also ordered the fighters, as did Australia, Canada, Israel, Italy, Japan, and Turkey. The number of countries taking part in the program was also expected to help keep costs in line. As the project began recording cost overruns, the Pentagon scaled back its order to 2,443, for a total of $382 billion. Some have called it the most expensive defense program in history—one that reveals massive cost overruns, a lack of clear strategic thought, and a culture in Washington that allows unchecked waste.

Defenders of the program say the way the government has calculated costs is at the heart of the overruns—a change in the scope and methods of government estimators rather than an actual escalation in costs. For the first time, the cost of lifetime modifications to the aircraft was included in the budget. Critics counter that when the $650 billion the Government Accountability Office estimates is needed to maintain the aircraft is added, the total costs reach $1 trillion. The Pentagon says the cost of maintaining the existing fleet of fighters each year is greater than the projected cost for the F-35s. Those costs will only go up as the fleet ages and the military struggles to repair fighters with metal fatigue, corrosion, and other age-related failures.

The US government's examination of its budget's defense-related expenses, such as those incurred in delivering the F-35s to the military, is one area where there is little agreement. The size of the military budget is examined in the following chapter of *Opposing Viewpoints: The US Deficit*. Other viewpoints explore whether cuts to the military budget would reduce national security, whether cuts to the defense budget can be made responsibly, and whether there is waste that can be cut in the defense budget.

> "US military spending now exceeds the spending of all other countries combined. . . . Some argue that all this spending has made us more secure, but all the evidence points in the opposite direction."

Cutting Defense Spending Will Reduce the Deficit and Increase National Security

David Morris

David Morris is a journalist and an economic advisor to local, state, and national governments. In the following viewpoint, he argues that the Pentagon is incompetent, wasteful, and corrupt, and that those who oppose cuts to military spending are ignoring the wishes of most Americans. Republicans, who Morris asserts are proponents of cutting government waste and government in general, operate contrary to their stated position when it comes to defense spending. In times when the focus should be on cutting the deficit, a program as wasteful and large as defense must be cut, Morris insists. The large US defense budget, Morris contends, encourages other countries to beef up their military pres-

David Morris, "Why Is the Most Wasteful Government Agency Not Part of the Deficit Discussion?," On the Commons, July 7, 2011. http://onthecommons.org/why-most-wasteful-government-agency-not-part-deficit-discussion. CC (Creative Commons) 2011 by On the Commons. (http://creativecommons.org/licenses/by/3.0/).

ence, decreasing US national security and consequently increasing spending to keep up with other countries. Further, Morris points out, as well as diverting funds from other pursuits that could support and stimulate the US economy, the military budget encourages and supports corrupt activities within the defense industry, the government, and the military.

As you read, consider the following questions:

1. What percentage of 2011 federal discretionary spending was accounted for by military spending, according to Morris?

2. How long does Morris say it has been since there was a complete audit of the Pentagon?

3. What percentage of retiring three- and four-star generals officials went to work as consultants or defense industry executives from 2004 to 2008, according to the viewpoint?

In all the talk about the federal deficit, why is the single largest culprit left out of the conversation? Why is the one part of government that best epitomizes everything conservatives say they hate about government—waste, incompetence, and corruption—all but exempt from conservative criticism?

Of course, I'm talking about the Pentagon. Any serious battle plan to reduce the deficit must take on the Pentagon. In 2011 military spending accounted for more than 58 percent of all federal discretionary spending and even more if the interest on the federal debt that is related to military spending were added. In the last ten years we have spent more than $7.6 trillion on military and homeland security according to the National Priorities Project.

In the last decade military spending has soared from $300 billion to $700 billion.

When debt ceilings and deficits seem to be the only two items on Washington's agenda, it is both revealing and tragic that both parties give a free pass to military spending. Representative Paul Ryan's much discussed [2011] Tea Party budget accepted [President Barack] Obama's proposal for a pathetic $78 billion reduction in military spending over 5 years, a recommendation that would only modestly slow the rate of growth of military spending.

Indeed, the Republican government battering ram appears to have stopped at the Pentagon door. This was evident early on. As soon as they took over the House of Representatives, Republicans changed the rules so that military spending does not have to be offset by reduced spending somewhere else, unlike any other kind of government spending. It is the only activity of government they believe does not have to be paid for, which brings to mind a bit of wisdom from one of their heroes, [social philosopher and political economist] Adam Smith. "Were the expense of war to be defrayed always by revenue raised within the year . . . wars would in general be more speedily concluded, and less wantonly undertaken."

Republican Opposition to Defense Cuts Is Hypocritical

The Tea Party revolution has only strengthened the Republican Party's resolve that the Pentagon's budget is untouchable. An analysis by the Heritage Foundation of Republican votes on defense spending found that Tea Party freshmen were even more likely than their Republican elders to vote against cutting any part of the military budget.

What makes the hypocrisy even more revealing is that the Pentagon turns out to be the poster child for government waste and incompetence.

In 2009 the Government Accountability Office (GAO) found "staggering" cost overruns of almost $300 billion in nearly 70 percent of the Pentagon's 96 major weapons. What's more, the programs were running, on average, 21 months behind schedule. And when they were completed, they provided less than they promised.

The Defense Logistics Agency had no use for parts worth more than half of the $13.7 billion in equipment stacked up in DOD [Department of Defense] warehouses in 2006 to 2008.

And these are only the tips of the military's misspending iceberg. We really don't know how much the Pentagon wastes because, believe it or not, there hasn't been a complete audit of the Pentagon in more than 15 years.

In 1994 the Government Management Reform Act required the inspector general of each federal agency to audit and publish the financial statements of their agency. The Department of Defense was the only agency that has been unable to comply. In fiscal year 1998 the Department of Defense used $1.7 trillion of undocumentable adjustments to balance the books. In 2002 the situation was even worse. CBS News reported that Secretary of Defense Donald Rumsfeld admitted, "we cannot track $2.3 trillion in transactions."

Imagine that a school district were to reveal that it didn't know where it spent its money. Now imagine the Republican response. Perhaps, "Off with their desktops!"

The Defense Department Is Not Held Accountable

How did Congress respond to DOD's delinquency? It gave it absolution and allowed it to opt out of its legal requirement. But as a sop [something given to pacify] to outraged public opinion, Congress required DOD to set a date when it would have its book sufficiently in order to be audited. Which the Pentagon dutiful did, and missed every one of the target dates. The latest is 2017 and DOD has already announced it will be unable to meet that deadline.

Adding insult to injury, last September, the GAO found that the new computer systems intended to improve the Pentagon's financial oversight are themselves nearly 100 percent or $7 billion over budget and as much as 12 years behind schedule!

"The Military-Industrial Bowl," cartoon by Pat Bagley, CagleCartoons.com. Copyright © 2012 by Pat Bagley and CagleCartoons.com. All rights reserved. Reproduced by permission.

The Pentagon is not just incompetent. It is corrupt. In November 2009 the Pentagon's Defense Contract Audit Agency (DCAA), the federal watchdog responsible for auditing oversight of military contractors, raised the question of criminal wrongdoing when it found that the audits that did occur were riddled with serious breaches of auditor independence. One Pentagon auditor admitted he did not perform detailed tests because, "The contractor would not appreciate it."

Why would the Pentagon allow its contractors to get away with fraud? To answer that question we need to understand the incestuous relationship between the Pentagon and its contractors that has been going on for years, and is getting worse. From 2004 to 2008, 80 percent of retiring three- and four-star officers went to work as consultants or defense industry executives. Thirty-four out of 39 three- and four-star generals and admirals who retired in 2007 are now working in defense industry roles—nearly 90 percent.

Generals are recruited for private sector jobs well before they retire. Once employed by the military contractor, the general maintains a Pentagon advisory role.

"In almost any other realm it would seem a clear conflict of interest. But this is the Pentagon where . . . such apparent conflicts are a routine fact of life," an in-depth investigation by the *Boston Globe* concluded.

US military spending now exceeds the spending of all other countries combined. Knowledgeable military experts argue that we can cut at least $1 trillion from the Pentagon budget without changing its currently expressed mission. But a growing number believe that the mission itself is suspect. Economic competitors like India and China certainly approve of our willingness to undermine our economic competitiveness by diverting trillions of dollars into war and weapons production. Some argue that all this spending has made us more secure, but all the evidence points in the opposite direction. Certainly our $2 trillion and counting military adventures in the Middle East and Afghanistan and Pakistan have won us few friends and multiplied our enemies.

Unrestrained Spending Threatens Stability and Security

Defense experts Gordon Adams and Matthew Leatherman, writing in the *Washington Post*, offer another argument against unrestrained military spending.

> Countries feel threatened when rivals ramp up their defenses; this was true in the Cold War, and now it may happen with China. It's how arms races are born. We spend more, inspiring competitors to do the same—thus inflating defense budgets without making anyone safer. For example, [Defense Secretary Robert] Gates observed in May [2010] that no other country has a single ship comparable to our 11 aircraft carriers. Based on the perceived threat that this fleet poses, the Chinese are pursuing an anti-ship ballistic

missile program. US military officials have decried this "carrier-killer" effort, and in response we are diversifying our capabilities to strike China, including a new long-range bomber program, and modernizing our carrier fleet at a cost of about $10 billion per ship.

For tens of millions of Americans real security comes not from fighting wars on foreign soil but from not having to worry [about] losing their house or their job or their medical care. As Joshua Holland, columnist for AlterNet, points out, 46 states faced combined budget shortfalls this year of $130 billion, leading them to fire tens of thousands of workers and cut off assistance to millions of families. Just the supplemental requests for fighting in Iraq and Afghanistan this year were $170 billion.

What is perhaps most astonishing of all is that cutting the military budget is wildly popular. Even back in 1995, when military spending was only a fraction of its present size, a poll by the Program on International Policy Attitudes reported that 42 percent of the US public felt that defense spending was too high and a majority of Americans were convinced that defense spending "has weakened the US economy and given some allies an economic edge."

This March Reuters released a new poll that found the majority of Americans support reducing defense spending.

The next time you hear Republicans insist they want to ferret out government waste and reduce spending and stamp out incompetence ask them why the one part of government that exemplifies everything they say is wrong with government is the one part of government they embrace most heartily.

> *"Defense spending is unlike other spending, because protecting the nation is a government's first job. It's in the Constitution, as highways, school lunches and Social Security are not."*

The Dangerous Debate over Cutting Military Spending

Robert J. Samuelson

Robert J. Samuelson is an author and journalist who writes a weekly economics column for the Washington Post. *In the following viewpoint, he argues that while spending on the wars in Iraq and Afghanistan has contributed to the deficit and that the deficit will automatically become lower when the wars are over, the amount of difference it will make will be much, much smaller than is popularly believed or reported. He says that the United States spends much less on the military than it did in the 1950s and 1960s, when the country had less money, countering arguments that America cannot afford its military. He also maintains that when those arguing for cuts claim that the United States' expenditures are so much larger than other countries' on military, they fail to take into account that it costs the United States far more to pay for its troops, contractors, and supplies than it*

Robert J. Samuelson, "The Dangerous Debate over Cutting Military Spending," *Washington Post*, October 30, 2011. http://www.washingtonpost.com/opinions/the-dangerous-debate-over-cutting-military-spending/2011/10/28/gIQAnPWEXM_story.html. Copyright © 2011 by the Washington Post. All rights reserved. Reproduced by permission.

does other countries. Further, he adds, countries such as China have greater manpower in their military than the United States. Samuelson concludes that any waste or inefficiency in the Pentagon budget has already been addressed through major cuts, and further cuts to an already streamlined military would hamper its ability to effectively address terrorism and other threats to national security.

As you read, consider the following questions:

1. How many combat battalions did the US Army have in 1990, according to Samuelson?

2. How much larger is China's military manpower than the United States', according to the viewpoint?

3. When does Samuelson say was the last time defense spending was below 3 percent of national income?

We shouldn't gut defense. A central question of our budget debates is how much we allow growing spending on social programs to crowd out the military and, in effect, force the United States into a dangerous, slow-motion disarmament.

People who see military cuts as an easy way to reduce budget deficits forget that this has already occurred. From the late 1980s to 2010, the number of America's armed forces dropped from 2.1 million men and women to about 1.4 million. The downsizing—the "peace dividend" from the end of the Cold War—was not undone by the wars in Iraq and Afghanistan. In 1990, the Army had 172 combat battalions, the Navy 546 ships and the Air Force 4,355 fighters; today, those numbers are 100 battalions, 288 ships and 1,990 fighters.

True, Iraq and Afghanistan raised defense budgets. As these wars conclude, lower spending will shrink overall deficits. But the savings will be smaller than many expect because the costs—though considerable—were smaller than they thought.

From fiscal year 2001 to 2011, these wars cost $1.3 trillion, says the Congressional Budget Office. That's 4.4 percent of the $29.7 trillion of federal spending over those years. In fiscal 2011, the cost was about $159 billion, 12 percent of the deficit ($1.3 trillion) and 4 percent of total spending ($3.6 trillion).

Three bogus arguments are commonly made to rationalize big military cuts.

First, we can't afford today's military.

Not so. How much we spend is a political decision. In the 1950s and 1960s, when the country was much poorer, 40 percent to 50 percent of the federal budget routinely went to defense, representing 8 to 10 percent of our national income. By 2010, a wealthier America devoted only 20 percent of federal spending and 4.8 percent of national income to the military. Spending on social programs replaced military spending, but that shift has gone too far.

Second, we spend so much more than anyone else that cutbacks won't make us vulnerable.

In 2009, U.S. defense spending was six times China's and 13 times Russia's, according to estimates from the Stockholm International Peace Research Institute. The trouble with these numbers is that they don't truly adjust for differences in income levels. U.S. salary and procurement costs are orders of magnitude higher than China's, for example. But China's military manpower is about 50 percent greater than ours, and it has a fighter fleet four-fifths as large. This doesn't mean that China's military technology yet equals ours, but differences in reported spending are wildly misleading.

Third, the Pentagon has so much inefficiency and waste that sizable cuts won't jeopardize our fighting capability.

Of course there is waste and inefficiency. These are being targeted in the $450 billion of additional cuts over 10 years— beyond savings from Iraq and Afghanistan—that President Obama and Congress agreed to this year. Former defense secretary Robert Gates had already cut major programs including the F-22 stealth fighter that he judged unneeded. Savings can be had from overhauling Tricare, the generous health insurance program for service members and retirees. But like most bureaucratic organizations, the Pentagon will always have some waste. It's a myth that it all can be surgically removed without weakening the military.

Defense spending is unlike other spending, because protecting the nation is a government's first job. It's in the Constitution, as highways, school lunches and Social Security are not. We should spend as much as needed, but that amount is never clear. Even in the Cold War, when the Soviet Union's capabilities were intensively analyzed, there was no scientific and exact number.

Now our concept of national security—and demands on the military—has become expansive and murky. Aside from preventing attacks on the homeland, goals include: stopping terrorism; countering China's rise; combating cyber warfare; limiting nuclear proliferation (Iran, North Korea); averting the loss or theft of nuclear weapons (Pakistan?); safeguarding sea routes and some major oil producers; and providing humanitarian assistance in major natural disasters.

By itself, defense spending does not ensure that our national power will be wisely or effectively deployed. This depends on our civilian and military leaders. But squeezing defense will limit these leaders' choices and expose U.S. troops to greater risk. Those who advocate deep cuts need to specify which goals—combating cyber warfare, countering China, fighting terrorism—should be curtailed. Would that be good for us? The world?

America's military advantage stems from advanced technology and intensive troop training. Obama repeatedly pledges to maintain America's strength, but the existing cuts may do otherwise. Even before these, defense spending was headed below 3 percent of national income, the lowest level since 1940.

The need to maintain an adequate military is another reason why spending on social programs needs to be cut and taxes need to be raised.

"*There is scarcely an economic policy is- sue before the Congress that does not affect U.S. national security. Likewise, there is scarcely a national security policy issue that does not affect the economy.*"

Cutting Defense Spending Should Be Done Carefully to Preserve National Security

Dick K. Nanto and Mindy R. Levit

Dick K. Nanto is a specialist in industry and trade, and Mindy R. Levit is an analyst in public finance, both for the Congressional Research Service. In the following viewpoint, the authors illustrate the close and complex relationship between the US economy—including the federal deficit—and national security. Threats posed by terrorism, the global financial crisis, and the rise of a global marketplace, the authors assert, present new na- tional security concerns that call for an appropriate and carefully crafted approach to spending and deficit reduction. They high- light the importance of establishing a sound fiscal policy and the responsibility of Congress to protect national security by taking action to ensure financial stability.

Dick K. Nanto and Mindy R. Levit, "Economics and National Security: Issues and Im- plications for US Policy," Congressional Research Service, January 4, 2011, pp. 1, 2, 4–6, 9–11, 14–15, 77. http://www.fas.org/sgp/crs/natsec/R41589.pdf

As you read, consider the following questions:

1. What does the figure provided in the viewpoint categorize under "hard power" and "soft power"?

2. Defense expenditures account for what percentage of the US federal budget, according to the authors?

3. What did fifty-seven members of Congress call on the National Commission on Fiscal Responsibility and Reform to do in a letter dated October 13, 2010, according to the viewpoint?

U.S. national security underpins the system in which Americans live. National security is essential to an environment and geographical space in which people can reside without fear. It consists, first, of physical security on both the international and domestic sides. This includes protection from threats external to the country and safety in the homeland. These generally are accomplished through hard power and homeland security efforts. Second, it consists of economic security—the opportunity and means for people to provide for their own well-being under an economic system that is vibrant, growing, and accessible. Third, U.S. national security involves outreach through soft power in an attempt to win the "hearts and minds" of people across the globe. Soft power complements hard power, and, in some cases, may substitute for it. Also, the myriad links between governments, businesses, and people across national borders means that American security increasingly depends on countries and activities in far-flung places on the globe.

Traditionally, the economy entered into the national security debate through four issues: the defense industrial base, base closures and program cuts, international economic sanctions, and export controls. These issues still garner much of the attention from the vantage point of the military. From the point of view of the nation as a whole, however, economic security takes on a broader meaning. . . .

Terrorist and Economic Threats Loom Large in National Security Debate

In the United States, the renewed public debate over national security appears to be generated primarily by three global changes. The first is the nature of the external threat to physical security—the rise of terrorism and militant Islam. The second is the aftermath of the global financial crisis, particularly the large federal budget deficit and slow rate of recovery. The third is the growing presence of emerging nations, such as China, India, and Brazil, and the shift of economic power toward them. These changes have created gaps and trade-offs that arguably are undermining the sense of security of Americans. Some may say, "What good is protection from a future threat, when I am unemployed because my job just went to China?" Others may say, "What good is a high salary, if I am dead in a terrorist attack?"

This debate over national security reaches deep into the fiber of American society. It is not merely political theater, and it is receiving a fillip [boost] by the weakened U.S. economy. A vibrant, growing, and dominant economy can hide a multitude of problems. Even though wealth and economic means cannot guarantee U.S. security, it can buy a comfortable sort of insecurity.

The economic issue of the day now centers on what measures to take to return the economy to its long-term growth path and reduce the gap between the potential and actual levels of U.S. gross domestic product. If the economy were to grow faster, many of the constraints on the federal budget would be eased. There are two major schools of thought on this matter. The Keynesian [based on the economic theories of John Maynard Keynes] approach to growth is to continue government deficit spending through the recession and initial recovery phase in order to offset lower consumption by households and reduced levels of investment by businesses. When the economy recovers, the deficit can be reduced. The supply-side approach is to cut the federal budget deficit now because deficits may discourage investment by causing uncertainty about future policy changes that will be needed to restore fiscal balance. The supply-side approach also attempts to keep taxes on entrepreneurs low in order to induce them to invest more in productive capacity and create more jobs. Each approach recognizes that the long-term security of the nation depends greatly on having a vibrant and growing economy.

Congress plays a major role in each element of national security. Whether it be policies dealing with the military, economy, budget, education, economic growth, technology, international relations, or opening markets abroad, Congressional action is essential. Not only does Congress provide funding for these elements of national security, but it provides oversight, defines the scope of U.S. action, and provides a crucible in which U.S. policies are debated and often determined. Congress allocates the resources to respond to national security threats, and in so doing it plays a part in determining the relative strength of hard and soft power options and the roles individual agencies will play. . . .

Figure 1 provides a simplified overview of how the economy enters into national security considerations. National security is sought through a combination of hard power, soft power, and economic opportunity. The economy underpins each of these by providing funding, human and other resources, capital, products, and an appealing culture and economic model. The operation of the economy, in turn, relies on government fiscal, monetary, and industrial policies; on the quality and quantity of human resources; on progress in science and technology; and on the global economy through trade and capital flows. . . .

Figure 1: The Economy and National Security

National Security

Physical Security   Economic Security   National Values

Hard Power   Economic Opportunity   **Soft Power**
National Defense   Jobs, Income Security   Diplomacy, Aid
Homeland Security   Culture, Media

U.S. Economy

Defense Industrial Base   **Competitive U.S. Industries**

Fiscal, Monetary   Human Resources   Innovation   World Economy
and Industrial   Education   Science   Trade
Policies   Immigration   Technology   Capital Flows

Source: Congressional Research Service

TAKEN FROM: Dick K. Nanto and Mindy R. Levit, "Economics and National Security: Issues and Implications for US Policy," Congressional Research Service, January 4, 2011.

The Federal Deficit and Military Spending

The expectation is that the current and projected growth in the national debt is not sustainable and, given the slow recovery from the financial crisis, the nation is facing a period of increased austerity that will compel deep cuts in the federal budget. The question is when those cuts should be made and to what extent the Pentagon is to be included or exempt from budget cuts. In August 2010, Admiral Mike Mullen, Chairman of the Joint Chiefs of Staff, stated that the national debt is the single biggest threat to national security.

In theory, the budget for the national security community, including the military and homeland security, should be sufficient to address foreign threats, defend the homeland, prevail in ongoing wars, and help define and advance U.S. interests abroad, including, to a certain extent, projecting U.S. democratic values and human rights. In practice, there is considerable disagreement on how best to address these tasks and the ways and means necessary to carry them out. Without concurrence on the tasks, one can hardly expect a public policy consensus on the optimal size of the military budget and whether the amount being spent is too great or too small. The line of reasoning in the public debate, therefore, tends to be that the military budget is either too large or too small relative to what the country can afford, to past expenditures, to the overall federal budget, to what is spent on other programs, or to what other nations spend. Another line of reasoning is that the military budget also is too large or too small relative to current war-fighting needs, to rising threats from non-state actors (such as terrorists) or from states with nuclear weapon programs (such as North Korea and Iran), or for its participation in alleviating the effects of natural disasters (such as earthquakes, tsunamis, infectious diseases, or climate change).

U.S. defense expenditures account for nearly $700 billion in annual budget outlays, including some $400 billion in contracts for goods and services. The impact on U.S. gross domestic product exceeds $1 trillion. U.S. defense expenditures are roughly equal to those of the next 14 countries combined, account for about 20% of the U.S. federal budget, and comprise an estimated 4.9% of U.S. gross domestic product. . . .

In 2010, Defense Secretary Robert Gates called for significant cuts in defense spending. He has outlined some details of his plans to save $100 billion over the next five years. This includes new guidelines on how the Pentagon buys goods for services with more fixed price contracts, cutting overhead, gaining efficiency, and closing the Joint Forces Command in Norfolk, Virginia. . . . Secretary Gates, however, has warned against sharp reductions in military spending, arguing that such cuts would be "catastrophic" to national security.

In October 2010, the Heritage Foundation, American Enterprise Institute [for Public Policy Research], and the Foreign Policy Initiative issued a report claiming that the arguments frequently made for Pentagon spending cuts are false and that the Pentagon is actually underfunded given the need for comprehensive military modernization and to prepare fully for the wars of the future. The argument rests primarily on the global reach and expanding responsibilities of the U.S. military; the need to update military hardware; and the fact that spending on entitlements, Social Security, Medicare, and Medicaid has outstripped that of the Pentagon. The report noted that even if Pentagon spending of about $700 billion were eliminated entirely, it would only halve the fiscal deficit of around $1.3 trillion and hardly put a dent into the $13.6 trillion national debt. The report was followed by an op-ed piece by the heads of the three authoring organizations that argued that a strong military is necessary to keep the peace, and peace is required for global prosperity. Hence, military spending is not a net drain on the U.S. economy.

A counterview of the debate has been put forward by the Sustainable Defense Task Force. On June 11, 2010, it issued a report that concluded that at a time of "growing concern over federal deficits, it is essential that all elements of the federal budget be subjected to careful scrutiny. The Pentagon budget should be no exception." The report presents options that the task force argues could save up to $960 billion between 2011 and 2020. The options include recommendations that focus on cutting programs based on unreliable or unproven technologies, missions and capabilities with poor cost-benefit relationships, capabilities that mismatch or overmatch current and emerging challenges, and management reforms. Based partly on this report, a group of 57 members of Congress sent a letter to the [National] Commission on Fiscal Responsibility [and Reform, dated October 13, 2010,] calling on the commission to subject military spending to the same rigorous scrutiny that nonmilitary spending was to receive and to do it in a way that would not endanger national security.

On December 1, 2010, the commission released its proposals to reduce the budget deficit. These proposals included $828 billion in deficit reduction between 2012 and 2015 through cuts in discretionary spending, tax reform, health care cost containment, mandatory savings, Social Security reform, and changes in the budget process. In particular, the commission recommended that both security and non-security discretionary spending be cut by an equal percentage. Since security spending is twice as large as non-security discretionary spending, equal percentage cuts imply that the amount of cuts in security spending would be twice as large as that in non-security spending. . . .

Reducing the Federal Budget Deficit

The federal budget is currently on an unsustainable path over the next several decades. This is primarily due to the impending retirement of baby boomers, rising life expectancy, and the increasing cost of medical care. Under current policies, federal debt, as a consequence of long-term and persistent budget deficits, is projected to grow to levels that may threaten the government's ability to meet its security and non-security obligations. As part of the 2010 National Security Strategy, President [Barack Obama] calls for achieving long-term fiscal sustainability. To accomplish this goal, he calls for creating a responsible federal budget that reduces the budget deficit by making the best use of taxpayer dollars and working with global partners and institutions.

Most budget analysts agree that deficit reduction is key over the long term in order to stabilize the economy and establish sound fiscal policy. However, the question over the short to medium term is how to ensure the continuation of economic recovery, while at the same time providing indications that the administration and Congress are committed to

The United States Can Defend Its Interests with a Smaller Military

As we look beyond the wars in Iraq and Afghanistan—and the end of long-term nation building with large military footprints—we'll be able to ensure our security with smaller conventional ground forces. We'll continue to get rid of outdated Cold War–era systems so that we can invest in the capabilities that we need for the future, including intelligence, surveillance and reconnaissance, counterterrorism, countering weapons of mass destruction and the ability to operate in environments where adversaries try to deny us access.

So, yes, our military will be leaner, but the world must know the United States is going to maintain our military superiority with armed forces that are agile, flexible and ready for the full range of contingencies and threats. . . .

I want to close with a word about the defense budget that will flow from this strategy. . . . Some will no doubt say that the spending reductions are too big; others will say that they're too small. It will be easy to take issue with a particular change in a particular program. But I'd encourage all of us to remember what President [Dwight D.] Eisenhower once said—that "each proposal must be weighed in the light of a broader consideration: the need to maintain balance in and among national programs." After a decade of war, and as we rebuild the source of our strength—at home and abroad—it's time to restore that balance.

Barack Obama,
"Remarks by the President on the Defense Strategic Review,"
January 5, 2012. www.whitehouse.gov.

improving the long-term budget outlook. If a more sustainable fiscal path is not achieved, high budget deficits and the resulting high levels of federal debt could limit the government's flexibility in meeting its obligations or in responding to the emerging national needs. Ultimately, failing to take action to reduce the projected growth in the debt could potentially lead to future insolvency or government default. . . .

The U.S. Economy and National Security Are Intertwined

As is evident from the topics covered above, economics enters into national security considerations through a variety of ways. The economy plays a dual role of providing the resources to help ensure the physical security of Americans and of generating employment and income to help ensure the economic security of households. The economy also provides a model, culture, and other elements of soft power helpful in winning the hearts and minds of people around the world. There is scarcely an economic policy issue before the Congress that does not affect U.S. national security. Likewise, there is scarcely a national security policy issue that does not affect the economy.

"Even if the US government dramatically reduced the defense budget, America's overall security and ability to project power on a global scale would remain far in excess of any potential rivals."

The US Defense Budget Is Bloated and Can Be Easily Cut

Taylor Marvin

Taylor Marvin writes about economics and politics for a variety of publications. In the following viewpoint, he acknowledges that achieving the appropriate balance between fiscal responsibility and national security is complex and difficult, but that arguments against larger cuts to the US defense budget do not reflect modern realities. Instead of rising to meet resource needs necessitated by threats to national security, as has been the case in the past, Marvin asserts, the US defense budget has in recent years been increased without careful consideration whether increasing conventional military forces would be helpful in fighting terrorism or in countering the growth of other countries' militaries. He maintains that contrary to claims made by proponents of maintaining the current level of defense spending, the United States

Taylor Marvin, "Is Cutting US Military Spending Really a Threat?," *Click Rally Magazine*, August 24, 2011. Copyright © 2011 by Click Rally. All rights reserved. Reproduced by permission.

does in fact spend vastly more than it needs to defend its interests, outspends most other countries in the world on its military, and could, because of advances in technology and the changing nature of warfare, successfully compete in modern war theaters with a smaller budget.

As you read, consider the following questions:

1. What was the policy called "New Look," according to Marvin?

2. What entity spends 67 percent of the total world defense budget, according to the viewpoint?

3. What percentage of its GDP does Marvin say Israel spends on defense, and why?

While discussions of the budget deficit have been common in US politics for the last 20 years, the 2010 midterm elections and emergence of the Tea Party have drawn unprecedented attention to demands that the US government dramatically reduce spending and shrink the federal debt. Unusually, these calls for reducing government spending have reached the Pentagon—while military spending has historically been held sacred by congressional Republicans, recently policy makers from both sides of American politics have called for reducing the US defense budget.

To many American politicians' commentators, this debate is dangerous. A spokesman for Senator Joe Lieberman recently bemoaned the looming cuts, fearing the debt package would "disproportionately cut defense spending and result in unacceptably high risk to our national security." In the *Weekly Standard*, William Kristol claimed cutting the Pentagon budget would make it "hard for the U.S. to remain the sole superpower," and the decision to include defense cuts in the debt austerity package was "the best day the Chinese ever had." Defense Secretary Leon Panetta—who was appointed with the expectation that his time in the White House Office of Management and Budget would help him smooth cuts to Pentagon spending—echoed these concerns, warning that "we cannot allow that effort to go so far and cut so deep that it jeopardizes our ability to deal with the other very real and very serious threats we face around the world."

The Appropriate Balance of Spending and Military Deterrence Is Hard to Achieve

Some degree of defense cuts are coming—the sheer size of the deficit necessitates shrinking the federal budget, and the Pentagon is too big a piece of the federal pie to avoid the reach of government austerity. Some of the criticisms of reducing the US defense budget are valid: Secretary Panetta's warning focused on the effects of across-the-board rather than targeted military cuts, which he insists will be more damaging to the overall capabilities of the US military than cutting individual missions. This argument is convincing, and should be heeded: Rather than attempting to cut a certain percentage across the entire Pentagon, lawmakers should be willing to make difficult choices and recognize that inflicting cuts on the military necessitates asking it to do less. However, broader criticisms of any reductions in US military spending are less convincing.

The core argument of defenders of the US military budget is that some level of defense spending is necessary to provide the security that permits American freedom and economic prosperity. The core premise of this argument is credible—the benefits of defense spending extend beyond assets that are actually used in combat. However, even if defense assets are never actually used in warfare, they provide a tangible benefit by deterring military aggression. While the United States faces close to zero risk of an open foreign invasion, high levels of American defense spending likely do deter attacks on US interests overseas. Finding the optimal level of deterrence is difficult. Ideally, the United States would spend the minimum amount necessary to deter potential rivals and no more. Of course, this type of simple cost calculation doesn't work in the real world: Optimizing deterrence spending requires balancing the costs of building a credible military deterrence and the monetary benefits of protecting US interests, two variables that are difficult to accurately estimate.

Despite the difficulty of optimizing the costs and benefits of deterrence, the US military does play an important role in protecting US interests. Often, critics of American military spending will dismiss conventional forces' contribution to the US deterrence force, arguing that the United States' extensive nuclear weapons stockpiles are enough to deter any attack on the United States. Unfortunately, this is wishful thinking. While nuclear weapons are useful for deterring major attacks on the United States, their sheer destructive power doesn't allow for variable responses to varied threats. Literally, because nuclear weapons are an all-or-nothing response, the threat to use them is not credible in most circumstances. The United States has experimented with reliance on nuclear weapons before: During the early years of the Cold War [hostility that developed after World War II between the United States and the Soviet Union, also known as the Union of Soviet Socialist Republics (USSR)], President [Dwight D.] Eisenhower, concerned about the affordability of the massive US military budget, drew down defense spending and planned to rely almost exclusively on nuclear weapons to deter a Soviet invasion of Western Europe. Unfortunately, this policy—termed "New Look"—was largely unsuccessful: While the US and European nuclear arsenals did deter a Soviet invasion, they were not enough to deter less dramatic threats to other US interests around the world. The Soviets knew that the US would not be prepared to initiate World War III for anything short of an open invasion of Europe, so the US nuclear force was unable to deter Soviet-inspired actions against peripheral US interests, like the invasion of South Korea. Successive US presidents abandoned the strategy of absolute reliance on nuclear deterrence. While the threat of the Soviet Union has vanished, this logic remains: The understandable American reluctance to destroy humanity means that nuclear weapons are not an effective military deterrence, and some level of conventional military spending remains necessary.

Defense Spending Is Far Greater than Actual Threats Warrant

However, US military spending far exceeds the level necessary to deter foreign aggression, even against peripheral US interests. Some of this excess is justified: If America wishes to fight long foreign wars and lead international humanitarian military interventions, the Pentagon budget must support these missions. Despite this, American defense spending is ultimately vastly disproportionate to its core requirements. The US Navy is a good example of this excess. America currently fields eleven aircraft carriers. Russia possesses one, a Cold War relic vastly less capable than its American counterparts. Despite Chinese naval ambitions in the western Pacific, China has struggled to refit an abandoned Soviet carrier, the ex-*Varyag*, for combat, and the introduction of modern indigenous Chinese carriers is likely decades off. It is not unreasonable to suppose that America's deterrence value would not be diminished if budget cuts forced the Navy to reduce the US carrier fleet. While a reduction in the number of US carrier battle groups would significantly reduce the number of theaters the US could exert military control over at any given time, this would likely not make US military threats less credible; that is, China would not be marginally more likely to invade Taiwan if the US fielded only seven six-billion-dollar supercarriers. Because the capabilities of all US military branches are so far beyond the minimum necessary to maintain an effective deterrence, even if the US government dramatically reduced the defense budget, America's overall security and ability to project power on a global scale would remain far in excess of any potential rivals.

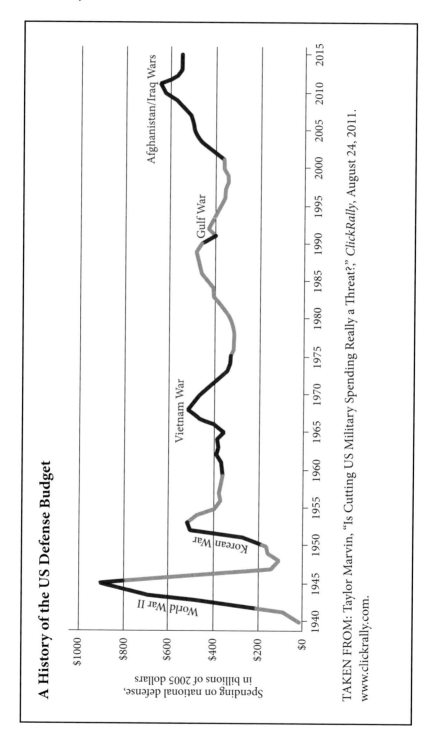

A History of the US Defense Budget

Spending on national defense, in billions of 2005 dollars

World War II

Korean War

Vietnam War

Gulf War

Afghanistan/Iraq Wars

1940 1945 1950 1955 1960 1965 1970 1975 1980 1985 1990 1995 2000 2005 2010 2015

$0 $200 $400 $600 $800 $1000

TAKEN FROM: Taylor Marvin, "Is Cutting US Military Spending Really a Threat?," *ClickRally*, August 24, 2011. www.clickrally.com.

Despite its real value as a credible deterrence, US spending on conventional forces are not based on the real security challenges facing the United States. In the last decade, US military spending in real terms has exploded. . . .

Generally, the defense budget has historically been set based on the real requirements of external threats: In the post-war era it increased rapidly at the start of the Cold War, fell during the détente period of the US-Soviet relationship initiated by President [Richard] Nixon, rose again during the 1980s, and fell slowly after the disintegration of the USSR. However, in the aftermath of the September 11th attacks [referring to the September 11, 2001, attacks on the United States] real spending rose again, surpassing the Cold War high by the late 2000s. This increase is not reflected by the defense challenge facing the United States in the 21st century. Despite the horrendous costs of the September 11th attacks, it strains credibility to argue that defending against Islamic terrorism requires significantly higher defense expenditures than deterring Soviet expansion. During the Cold War, the United States faced a technologically advanced and militarily experienced adversary that credibly threatened to overwhelm Western Europe, and whose military assets—airplanes, tanks, and men—were often more numerous than NATO's [North Atlantic Treaty Organization's]. While the threat of Islamic terrorism is real, the experience of the last decade demonstrates that it is not a threat that can be defeated or deterred by high levels of defense spending or conventional military forces.

Of course, terrorism is not the only security threat the United States faces in the near future. China's explosive growth as a world power and the expanding defense budgets of western Pacific countries all have the potential to pose serious threats to world stability and US security in the near future. Unlike terrorism, these potential threats require expensive naval and air assets to counter. This is often seen as an argument for preserving, or even raising, the US defense budget. However, the emergence of near-peer future competitors is not a convincing rational for costly US military spending, simply because an overwhelming share of world military spending belongs to either the US or firm US allies. . . .

NATO spends 67% of the total world defense budget, while Russia and China combined spend only 11.5%. Of course, the Chinese defense budget is increasing, and the Chinese economy has the ability to support a dramatic rise in military spending. However, the sheer size of the US fiscal lead above its rivals challenges the plausibility of arguing that any cuts to the Defense Department budget are dangerous. The US could halve its defense budget—a move few consider remotely plausible—and still outspend the rest of NATO combined.

The enormous size of the US military spending lead over all potential rivals is a strong argument that reducing the Defense Department budget would not be dangerous. However, ideological opponents of reducing defense spending often attempt to obscure this lead by pointing out that US military spending is actually fairly low as a percentage of total GDP [gross domestic product]. This argument is technically true but misleading. This does not deter its proponents: Sarah Palin [Republican vice presidential candidate in the 2008 election] has endorsed this view, once incredulously asking supporters if they knew "the U.S. actually only ranks 25th worldwide on defense spending as a percentage of GDP?" At face value, this statistic is troubling: How can we be assured of America's safety if our military spending is comparably so low? Of course, it isn't that simple. It is true that at under 5% of GDP American defense spending ranks at 25th in the world. However, nearly all countries that rank above US military spending as a percent of their total economy are tiny, impoverished, nonindustrial nations: Oman, Eritrea, the Maldives . . . none of these high spenders are exactly military behemoths. Overall, nations that spend over 4% of GDP on defense are either those facing extraordinary security situations (Israel) or poor countries with misguided spending priorities.

In fact, this trend continues for those ranked below the US in terms of spending as percent of GDP: The next highest fractional spending rich democracy is Australia, trailing at 43rd. Any way you look at the data, the US spends an enormous amount on defense, both in absolute and fractional terms. . . .

Deficit Reduction Must Include Defense

Any realistic effort to reduce the US federal deficit must include defense cuts. US defense spending is one of the largest individual components of the US federal budget—in 2010, the Department of Defense spent $689 billion, or roughly 20% of the federal budget, a percentage surpassed only by Social Security and medical entitlements. The federal budget is limited, and every dollar spent on defense is a dollar that can't be spent somewhere else. Secretary Panetta is aware of the conflict between social and military spending, remarking in an interview with reporters August 4th [2011] that government budget cuts should come from nondiscretionary entitlement programs like Social Security and Medicare, not the Pentagon. On its surface, Secretary Panetta's argument appears convincing. The United States currently spends twice the OECD [Organisation for Economic Co-Operation and Development] average on health care for substandard results, so clearly reforms in the enormously inefficient government health care programs like Medicare and Medicaid could free up funds for the military. However, inefficiency in other federal programs is not an argument for a blank check to the Pentagon. The main benefit of defense spending cuts would not be transferring these funds to other federal departments but removing them from the budget altogether. Recently both voters and politicians have become more cognizant of the fundamental unsustainability of the federal budget deficit. While America's budget woes cannot be remedied solely through military spending cuts (the projected constant rise in public medical costs are a much greater threat to America's long-term fiscal health than the Defense Department's budget), any credible plan to reduce US spending must include the Pentagon, which consumes a greater share of the federal budget than all non-defense discretionary spending combined. Commentators who claim to be fiscally conservative while categorically rejecting a reduction in military spending do not understand this fundamental truth.

Similarly, arguments that defense cuts would threaten America's technological innovation are unconvincing. It is true that Pentagon spending sparks enormous technological advancements—many of the hallmarks of the modern era like the Internet, microchip and communications satellites all sprang from military-funded research, and military needs and acquisitions drive much of the cutting-edge technological research that the US leads the world in. However, this is a misleading argument for preserving the high Department of Defense budget. If anything, this reasoning harkens back to the older arguments used to justify the Apollo-era space exploration spending; while enormously expensive, the Apollo program was justified by the technological advances it produced. While it is true the space program produced many innovations, going to the moon wasn't a particularly efficient way to fund these technological advancements. If new technologies were an important goal of the space program, it is obviously much more efficient to just increase government research funding. The same logic applies to defense spending. If we value the products of military R&D [research and development], then it's much more efficient and cheaper to just fund interesting research rather than rely on weapons programs for technologies that will have civilian applications. Justifying military spending by pointing to its side benefits is technically correct but ultimately a poor argument.

Modern Wars Can Be Fought with Smaller Budgets

The American experiences in Somalia, Iraq and Afghanistan demonstrate that despite the US's vast military spending and unmatched capabilities America does not have the ability to decisively win the unconventional conflicts that characterize the modern era. However, this is not a convincing argument for a larger defense budget. The most expensive weapons in the military's budget are those that have the least relevance to the type of low-intensity wars the US has been fighting for the last two decades: the F-22, advanced communications nets, an airborne laser missile defense system . . . all of these weapons systems are built for a large conventional war with a powerful state opponent. Counterinsurgency is enormously expensive, but the tools to fight it are less so. While cutting the Pentagon budget would reduce America's effectiveness in a future war with China, a large future conflict with a near-peer rival remains unlikely, and the wisdom of spending vast amounts of limited fiscal resources preparing for a conflict lower defense spending appears perfectly capable of deterring is debatable. Of course, in a perfect world, America would build an overwhelming dominance against any potential adversary, no matter how improbable. But can the United States continue to spend trillions of dollars out of a finite and shrinking budget to prepare for a major war that is very likely to never come?

However, reducing the US defense budget would preserve the US's ability to fight the low-intensity conflicts that dominate modern headlines. It's often argued that this isn't an important consideration: After the trauma of the long wars in Iraq and Afghanistan, the United States is unlikely to involve itself in another low-intensity counterinsurgency. However, history doesn't support this theory. . . .

Additionally, in the last few decades the world has entered an era where technological advances lead to less, not greater, returns on military investment. In the 1950s the only way to deny a powerful enemy control of the air or sea was to challenge it on equal terms: Limiting an enemy air force's operational capability required billions of dollars of investment in a comparable air force. The same applied to sea and, to an extent, land power. However, technological advancements have reduced the investment needed to impede an enemy's dominance. In Vietnam, the North Vietnamese could not hope to challenge the might of the American Air Force but were able to use much cheaper surface-to-air missiles to prevent the Americans from fully exploiting their advantage. Similarly, poorer nations unable to fund a navy can use affordable technologies like anti-ship missiles to destroy a richer nation's billions of dollars of naval investment. In the modern world, while weak nations still cannot replace the dominance of powerful ones, advancing technologies allow them to deny the powerful from making use of their theater control. While massive defense spending is still a prerequisite to military power, it is becoming less relevant to the ability to exert control and achieve victory. Increasing the military budget is not the path to winning future wars, nor should we fear careful cuts in the Pentagon's massive budget.

| "Defense spending helped create the fiscal crisis facing our nation today, and defense cuts must be part of the solution. The president and Congress can continue a bipartisan tradition of restoring defense spending to sustainable, responsible levels."

Past Presidential Administrations Provide a Blueprint for Sustainable Defense Spending

Lawrence J. Korb, Laura Conley, and Alex Rothman

Lawrence J. Korb is a senior fellow at the Center for American Progress, a senior advisor to the Center for Defense Information, an adjunct professor at Georgetown University, was a senior fellow and director of national security studies at the Council on Foreign Relations, and served as assistant secretary of defense from 1981 through 1985. Laura Conley is a research associate and Alex Rothman is a special assistant, both at the Center for American Progress. In the following viewpoint, they argue that many presidents in past administrations have lowered military

Lawrence J. Korb, Laura Conley, and Alex Rothman, "A Return to Responsibility: What President Obama and Congress Can Learn About Defense Budgets from Past Presidents," Center for American Progress, July 2011. Copyright © 2011 by the Center for American Progress. All rights reserved. Reproduced by permission.

spending without the nation suffering the drastic consequences predicted by those who oppose cuts to the defense budget. The authors point out that the United States is spending $250 billion more per year than it did during the Cold War, and that arguments that this spending cannot be cut are easily refuted by looking at how presidents throughout modern US history have been able to lower defense spending during challenging financial times. The authors emphasize that historically cuts have been made with bipartisan cooperation under presidents of both political parties, and they make several recommendations for cuts that they assert can reduce defense spending to a sustainable level and still ensure national security.

As you read, consider the following questions:

1. By how much did President Richard Nixon cut the defense budget as he withdrew from Vietnam, according to the authors?

2. Why do the authors say that President Dwight D. Eisenhower doubled funding for research, development, test, and evaluation?

3. How much do the authors indicate reforming military health care would save through 2015?

Congress and the [Barack] Obama administration must get defense spending under control as the country faces large budget deficits and debt—especially since military spending did much to contribute to our budget problems. Total U.S. defense spending (in inflation-adjusted dollars) increased so much over the past decade that it reached levels not seen since World War II when the United States had 12 million people under arms and waged wars on three continents.

Some of this growth can be attributed to the wars in Iraq and Afghanistan. But the baseline or regular defense budget has also increased significantly. The baseline budget, which does not include funding for Iraq or Afghanistan, has grown in real terms for an unprecedented 13 straight years. It is now $100 billion more than what the nation spent on average during the Cold War [hostility that developed after World War II between the United States and the Soviet Union]. When war funding is added, we are now spending about $250 billion more per year than during the Cold War. This ballooning defense budget played a significant role in turning the budget surplus projected a decade ago into a massive deficit.

As the Obama administration and Congress try to agree on a deal to raise the debt limit—an agreement that will inevitably involve cutting some money from the budget—they should keep in mind that they can cut $100 billion in defense spending annually and still keep our military budget at the [President Ronald] Reagan administration's peak Cold War levels of approximately $580 billion (all numbers adjusted for inflation unless otherwise noted). Bringing the defense budget down to the levels that existed under Presidents [Dwight D.] Eisenhower, [Richard] Nixon, [George] H.W. Bush, and [Bill] Clinton would require reductions of $250 billion to $300 billion annually.

A History of Responsible Defense Budgets During Challenging Times

The question currently facing Congress and President Barack Obama—how much to spend on defense in times of large deficits or in the final years of a war—is not new. In fact, . . . presidents from both parties carried out significant reductions in the defense budget under similar circumstances since the end of World War II.

Presidents Richard Nixon and Bill Clinton needed to identify reasonable levels of defense expenditures as the United States transitioned from war spending to peacetime budgets, while President Ronald Reagan needed to control defense spending in the face of rising deficits. Presidents Dwight D.

Eisenhower and George H.W. Bush, like President Obama today, confronted both scenarios at once. . . .

Defense Cuts Have Historically Been a Bipartisan Effort

First, requesting fiscally responsible defense budgets has been historically a bipartisan effort:

- To keep a balanced budget, President Dwight D. Eisenhower, a five-star army general and lifelong Republican, slashed defense spending by 27 percent after the armistice that ended the Korean War.

- President Richard Nixon, also a Republican and Eisenhower's vice president, cut the defense budget by 29 percent as he withdrew from Vietnam.

- Between 1985 and 1998, the defense budget fell for 13 straight years as Presidents Reagan, Bush, and Clinton—two Republicans and a Democrat—brought spending down to more sustainable levels as the Cold War wound down.

No National Security Risks Have Been Created by Cuts in Defense

Second, previous spending reductions did not compromise U.S. national security or create a hollow military, despite claims to the contrary:

- The spending cuts usually attributed to President Clinton and, on occasion, President George H.W. Bush actually began during the Reagan administration's second term when the United States was still engaged in the Cold War. This smaller military drove the Taliban [a fundamentalist Islamic militia] out of Afghanistan in 2001 in a matter of weeks and successfully ousted Saddam Hussein from Iraq. It might have fared better in both conflicts in the long term had the George W. Bush administration not insisted on an inadequately light footprint in the early years of those wars.

• Presidents Eisenhower and Nixon balanced sensible budget cuts with investment in the future of the force. President Eisenhower cut the defense budget by 27 percent during his time in office, but he also doubled funding for research, development, test, and evaluation, or RDT&E, so the United States could maintain its technological edge over the Soviets. It was the Eisenhower military that convinced the USSR [Union of Soviet Socialist Republics, or Soviet Union] to back down in the Cuban Missile Crisis [a major confrontation between the United States and the Soviet Union over the presence of Soviet nuclear missiles in Cuba in 1962].

• President Nixon also substantially reduced defense spending. But he outlined a more significant role for the military reserves (the Total Force) to ensure a smaller active-duty force had the support it needed to be successful in future conflicts. He also instigated a plan for aircraft procurement known as the high-low mix, meaning the services would diversify their purchases among expensive advanced fighters and less costly but still very capable planes (F-15s and F-16s for the Air Force and F-14s and F/A-18s for the Navy and Marines). This strategy allowed the Pentagon to buy a sufficient number of fighters at an acceptable cost. The F-16s and F/A-18s are still in service today and were used extensively in the first and second Gulf wars, from 1990 to 1991 and 2003 to present, respectively, and the Kosovo conflict in 1999.

Sensible Reductions Are Possible

Third, the Obama administration can achieve large savings from sensible reductions in the defense budget because it is at an unprecedented level:

- The Obama administration inherited a defense budget far in excess of even President Reagan's peak Cold War spending. And the idea that budget cuts will result in a "hollow force" or be catastrophic—advanced by critics such as former defense secretaries Donald Rumsfeld and Robert Gates—simply does not stand up to historical scrutiny. The Obama administration and Congress could cut $150 billion from the administration's current budget request and still be at average Reagan levels. President Obama would need to reduce the budget by about 40 percent, or close to $300 billion, to reach the budget levels established by Presidents Eisenhower, Nixon, and Clinton.

With these lessons in mind, we recommend that the Obama administration implement the following list of defense cuts to transition to a responsible and sustainable level of defense spending. These reductions would allow the president to reduce defense spending by $400 billion through 2015 without compromising U.S. national security. . . .

- Redirect the Defense Department's planned efficiency savings to reduce the baseline defense budget ($133 billion through 2015).

- Roll back post–September 11 [referring to the September 11, 2001, attacks on the United States] efforts to grow the ground forces and reduce the number of civilian DOD [Department of Defense] personnel concomitant with the reduction in military end strength ($39.16 billion through 2015).

- Reduce active-duty troops in Europe and Asia by one-third ($42.5 billion through 2015).

- Cancel the V-22 Osprey program ($9.15 billion through 2015).

- Reform military health care ($42 billion through 2015).

- Limit procurement of the Virginia-class submarine and DDG-51 destroyer to one per year, and limit procurement of the littoral combat ship to two vessels per year ($20.04 billion through 2015).

- Cut procurement of the Navy and Marines F-35 Joint Strike Fighter variants ($16.43 billion through 2015).

- Institute an across-the-board reduction in research, development, test, and evaluation funding ($40 billion through 2015).

- Reform the military pay system as the 10th Quadrennial Review of Military Compensation recommends ($13.75 billion through 2015).

- Cancel procurement of the CVN-80 aircraft carrier and retire two existing carrier battle groups and associated air wings ($7.74 billion).

- Cut the U.S. nuclear arsenal to 311 operationally deployed strategic nuclear weapons ($33.72 billion).

Defense spending helped create the fiscal crisis facing our nation today, and defense cuts must be part of the solution. The president and Congress can continue a bipartisan tradition of restoring defense spending to sustainable, responsible levels as the United States winds down its involvement in Iraq and Afghanistan.

| *"The defense industry is due for significant change, and it will take more than cutting corporate expenses or the sale of underperforming businesses to achieve it."*

Reforming the Defense Industry Will Help Cut Defense Spending and the Deficit

August Cole

August Cole is a fellow at the American Security Project, where he focuses on defense industry issues. In the following viewpoint, he argues that reform within the defense industry should come from within the industry itself rather than imposed through drastic budget cuts as part of deficit reduction efforts. In addition to increasing efficiency and accountability across the board, Cole asserts, the defense industry must reduce significantly its emphasis on lobbying for government contracts and focus on instituting sound business practices that will attract investors and appeal to shareholders. By reforming itself, Cole concludes, the defense industry can preserve its own interests and protect the jobs and economic interests of the American people who depend on it.

August Cole, "Defense Companies Must Do More than Lobby Against Cuts," AOL Defense, September 30, 2011. http://defense.aol.com/2011/09/30/defense-companies-must-do-more-than-lobby-against-cuts. Copyright © 2011 by August Cole. All rights reserved. Reproduced by permission.

As you read, consider the following questions:

1. What does Cole say are the consequences of cutting hardware and research and development spending?

2. What member of the Super Committee said he'd rather resign from the group than agree to more defense cuts, according to the viewpoint?

3. Why does Cole say that lobbying has become a liability outside of Washington, DC?

This time it's different.

For more than a year, defense companies have taken measured steps to prepare for defense spending budget cuts. Many pruned corporate spending, sending fewer executives to foreign air shows. Some, like Lockheed Martin, even offered sweeping buyouts. Others even sold off headache-causing businesses, as Northrop Grumman Corp. did by spinning off its shipyards. . . .

These are significant moves for an industry that's had a strong financial run during the past decade but seems convinced it can hold its own as defense spending declines in the coming years.

It's not going to be enough.

So far, what the big defense companies have been doing is keeping pace with, or just a whisker ahead of, the politics of the moment. The Second to None pro-defense initiative, backed by the industry, is a predictable move that might work in ordinary times. After all, there is no immediate advantage to doing anything rash, like getting out of the defense market entirely. At least not yet. It may come to that for some firms if we revisit the shameful politicking seen during the debt-ceiling debacle this summer [2011].

Political Interests Make Possible Legal Reforms Precarious for the Industry

The defense industry is standing on a very high ledge. Like the Beltway [referring to Washington, DC] area itself, the industry has been through a post-9/11 [referring to the September 11, 2001, terrorist attacks on the United States] boom that echoes the dot-com bubble era of 1990s San Francisco. If there's any doubt, just count the number of European sports cars around the office towers in Tysons Corner [Virginia] or peruse Securities and Exchange Commission filings for the equity compensation of senior defense executives. The tech bubble burst quickly, given the nature of the equity markets at the time. The defense bubble is so far deflating slowly, not suddenly bursting given the nature of government contracting and the lock Washington lawmakers have on many weapons programs. While Americans are clearly occupied with the flagging economy, and not whether the Marine Corps should get its own version of the [F-35] Joint Strike Fighter, defense spending remains an important political club that Republicans can wield over Democrats. The two issues are intertwined because cutting hardware and research and development spending, as defense industry proponents keep pointing out, means losing jobs that are very hard or impossible to replace. Most major weapons programs count suppliers in all, or almost all, 50 states for a reason. There is a very good chance the members of the deficit "Super Committee" [referring to the Joint Select Committee on Deficit Reduction], itself a product of this summer's bare-knuckle political brawl, will succumb to these temptations and fail to come up with more than $1 trillion in broad federal budget cuts. Already, Ariz. Sen. Jon Kyl boasted he'd rather resign from the group than agree to more defense cuts. This kind of grandstanding will lead to certain chaos in the one area where fiscal sanity and political poise are needed most: defense. If the "Super Committee" failure triggers automatic cuts to government spending, what should

US Deputy Secretary of Defense Urges Defense Industry Buyers to Increase Affordability and Productivity

We do not have an arsenal system in the United States: The Department [of Defense] does not make most of our weapons or provide many nongovernmental services essential to war fighting—these are provided by private industry. Our industry partners are patriots as well as businessmen. . . . Most of the rest of the economy exhibits productivity growth, meaning that every year the buyer gets more for the same amount of money. So it should be in the defense economy. Increased productivity is good for both industry and government. So also is avoiding budget turbulence and getting more programs into stable production.

Ashton B. Carter,
Memorandum for Acquisition Professionals,
"Better Buying Power: Mandate for Restoring Affordability
and Productivity in Defense Spending,"
June 28, 2010. www.defense.gov.

have been a painful but necessary winnowing away of wasteful Pentagon programs and practices will become something ugly—and dangerous.

The defense industry is due for significant change, and it will take more than cutting corporate expenses or the sale of underperforming businesses to achieve it. Something more profound is under way, and the fight over the country's fiscal future may speed it along faster than anyone in the industry thinks is possible.

To remain strong as the defense bubble deflates, the sector's companies must take some uncomfortable steps. One of the most important is to recognize that their primary customer, the Pentagon, is a terrible role model when it comes to efficiency and accountability—the very qualities that will be needed most during the next decade. The industry needs to be its own best role model.

Focus on Shareholders Rather than Lobbying Government

Perhaps the toughest measure will be to back off from the costly lobbying and political influence in Washington that's now a hallmark of the industry. This has become a liability beyond the Beltway, making the industry's companies look like they can't compete on the merits of their work. Another crucial step is rebalancing shareholder interests against those of government customers. That will upset some big investors, but this is an era where utility-like performance in the aerospace sector is going to be increasingly attractive. After all, taxpayers increasingly eye each dollar of contractor corporate profit, wondering how much of that money was once theirs. This is an era of zero-sum game political and economic outcomes in Washington. The defense industry is now no different.

The country needs a strong defense industry, but it is time to redefine where that strength comes from. It should be defined by stronger partnerships with the Defense Department, less Beltway acrimony and reliable and consistent contract performance. What's needed most isn't easily measured: a willingness to embrace the change at hand. If the industry does not, the hangover from years of wasted taxpayer dollars and excessive political influence will soon undo the industry's fortunes—if draconian budget cuts don't do it first.

| "*The reality is that much of the world is free riding off the security provided by American military dominance.*"

America Can No Longer Afford to Keep the World Safe

Will Wilkinson

Will Wilkinson writes about American politics for the Economist *and other publications. In the following viewpoint, he argues that the US military has been providing security services to protect worldwide economic interests but can no longer afford to do so. He maintains that conservatives who resist slashing defense budgets and advocate slashing entitlement spending are not arguing based on facts, and in the case of their position on defense are undercutting their overall philosophy on shrinking government and cutting waste. If the United States were to cut its military to just what it needs to secure its own borders and interests, Wilkinson concludes, other countries would—and should—step in to protect other economic and security interests around the world.*

As you read, consider the following questions:

1. The US military budget is greater than the combined military budgets of what countries, according to Wilkinson?

Will Wilkinson, "Hands Off the Warfare State!," *The Economist*, October 4, 2010. Reproduced by permission.

2. How much was the US debt in 2008, according to Joseph E. Stiglitz and Linda Bilmes, as quoted by Wilkinson?

3. What amount per year of military spending does Wilkinson say should suffice, if the purpose of military spending is to secure a calm climate conducive to global trade?

Are they worried? When the presidents of [Washington,] DC's two most powerful conservative think tanks team up with America's most prominent cheerleader for war to jointly author a *Wall Street Journal* op-ed defending the United States' unfathomably colossal military budget, one suspects a bit of anxiety.

The folks of the Tea Party movement are clearly upset at what they see as out-of-control spending, and frequently express a desire to slash the size of government. A quick glance at the federal budget is enough to see that military spending is far and away the largest expense after Medicare and Social Security. That fact combined with the observation that America's titanic military budget is larger than the military budgets of China, Britain, France, Russia, Germany, Japan, Saudi Arabia, Italy, South Korea, Brazil, Canada, and Australia *combined* is more than enough to suggest to common sense that there's room here to cut a bit of fat.

But not so fast! According to AEI's [American Enterprise Institute for Public Policy Research's] Arthur Brooks, Heritage Foundation's Ed Feulner, and the *Weekly Standard*'s Bill Kristol, any attempt to shrink the big government of garrisons and guns will "make the world a more dangerous place, and . . . impoverish our future." Whose side are you on, Tea Partiers?

Messrs Brooks, Feulner, and Kristol assert that military spending "is neither the true source of our fiscal woes, nor an appropriate target for indiscriminate budget-slashing in a still-dangerous world". They aver that "anyone seeking to restore our fiscal health should look at entitlements first, not across-the-board cuts aimed at our men and women in uniform".

Cutbacks Are Needed Across the Board

This is bogus. Sure, Medicare and Social Security cost *more*, but spending on war and its infrastructure remains a titanic expense. The path from debt, whether for governments or families, is to cut back across the board. If you're in the red and you spend a ridiculous amount of your income on your porcelain egret collection, the fact that you spend even more on rent and student loan payments is obviously no excuse not to cut back on egret miniatures. And, in fact, America's martial profligacy [excessive military spending] is a "true source of our fiscal woes". According to Joseph [E.] Stiglitz and Linda Bilmes:

> There is no question that the Iraq war added substantially to the federal debt. This was the first time in American history that the government cut taxes as it went to war. The result: a war completely funded by borrowing. U.S. debt soared from $6.4 trillion in March 2003 to $10 trillion in 2008 (before the financial crisis); at least a quarter of that increase is directly attributable to the war. And that doesn't include future health care and disability payments for veterans, which will add another half-trillion dollars to the debt.

> As a result of two costly wars funded by debt, our fiscal house was in dismal shape even before the financial crisis—and those fiscal woes compounded the downturn.

America Does Not Need to Spend Money to Make Money or Keep Peace

Perhaps because they see the wrongheadedness of their line of defence, Messrs Brooks, Feulner, and Kristol retreat to the claim that in order to make money, America has to spend money:

Furthermore, military spending is not a net drain on our economy. It is unrealistic to imagine a return to long-term prosperity if we face instability around the globe because of a hollowed-out U.S. military lacking the size and strength to defend American interests around the world.

Global prosperity requires commerce and trade, and this requires peace. But the peace does not keep itself.

Again: completely shabby. The real question at issue here is how much military spending is necessary to keep the trade routes open, and how much of that the United States must kick in. By asserting, rather audaciously, that America's level of military spending is not a "net drain" on the economy, they imply the return on the marginal trillion is positive. I doubt it. The return on the three trillion blown on the war on Iraq, for example, is certainly much, much, much less than zero once the cost of removing financial and human capital from productive uses is taken into account. Also, if prosperity requires peace, it's utterly mysterious how *starting* expensive wars is supposed to help.

Other Nations Should Share the Burden of Providing Security

When thinking about peace as a global public good, it can help to recall that the United States is not the only country that benefits from it. Suppose the United States were to cut its military budget in half to something like the size of the combined budgets of the next five or six countries. This might not suffice if you're itching to invade Yemen, Iran, and who knows what else Mr Kristol's got his eye on. But if the argument is that the purpose of military spending is to secure a calm climate conducive to global trade, it's hard to believe $350 billion per annum [year] will not suffice. But let's say it doesn't, for the sake of argument. Will nations with an equally strong interest in keeping the peace simply faint on their divans

America Should Not Be the World's Policeman

Hundreds of thousands of our fighting men and women have been stretched thin all across the globe in over 135 countries—often without a clear mission, any sense of what defines victory, or the knowledge of when they'll be permanently reunited with their families.

Acting as the world's policeman and nation building weakens our country, puts our troops in harm's way, and sends precious resources to other nations in the midst of a historic economic crisis.

Taxpayers are forced to spend billions of dollars each year to protect the borders of other countries, while Washington refuses to deal with our own border security needs.

Ron Paul, "National Defense,"
Ron Paul 2012 Presidential Campaign Committee,
June 30, 2011. www.ronpaul2012.com.

whenever a commerce-threatening war breaks out? Of course not. Even the French are perfectly capable of keeping the sea lanes open.

The reality is that much of the world is free riding off the security provided by American military dominance. Were American taxpayers to refuse to bear so much of the burden of keeping the world safe for Danish container ships, other countries would surely step up. Furthermore, considerations of basic distributive fairness suggest they should.

So listen up Tea Partiers! Slashing military spending will not only shrink government and help put us on a path to fiscal responsibility while stripping unaccountable, fat-cat defence contractors of hundreds of billions in corporate welfare;

it will *also* strip foreigners, many of whom speak *ridiculous* languages, of large defence subsidies paid out of *your* pocket! What's not to love?

Messrs Brooks, Feulner, and Kristol have offered the Tea Party movement an excellent opportunity to show what it's really made of. Will it allow itself to be captured by Washington's establishment conservative elite? Will it follow the example of the American Enterprise Institute, the Heritage Foundation, and the *Weekly Standard* and fight, fight, fight for big government, just as long as it's big government bristling with the tools of conquest and mass death? Or will it recognise that war is the health of the state, the enemy of liberty, and the bane of humanity and stand up to the big-government Washington war machine?

I'm putting my money on capture. Never bet against Bill Kristol.

Periodical and Internet Sources Bibliography

The following articles have been selected to supplement the diverse views presented in this chapter.

David W. Barno, Nora Bensahel, and Travis Sharp	"How to Cut the Defense Budget Responsibly," *Foreign Affairs*, November 2, 2011.
David Callahan	"Paul Ryan's Weak Case for a Strong Defense," *The Great Debate*, March 22, 2012. http://blogs.reuters.com.
Colin Clark	"Defense Industry Comes Out Swinging: Don't Cut Us!," AOL Defense, September 14, 2011. http://defense.aol.com.
Helle Dale	"Don't Cut Defense to Fund State," *The Foundry*, May 24, 2011. http://blog.heritage.org.
Ezra Klein	"Can We Cut the Military Budget Without Harming Innovation?," *Washington Post*, January 7, 2012.
Richard Lardner	"Military Spending Waste: Up to $60 Billion in Iraq, Afghanistan War Funds Lost to Poor Planning, Oversight, Fraud," *Huffington Post*, August 30, 2011. www.huffingtonpost.com.
Michael O'Hanlon	"Cut Defense, but with Eye on These Threats," *USA Today*, November 21, 2011.
Andrew Quinn	"Hillary Clinton Says Deficit Sends Message of Weakness," Reuters, September 8, 2010. www.reuters.com.
Gerald F. Seib	"Deficit Balloons into National-Security Threat," *Wall Street Journal*, February 2, 2010.
Loren Thompson	"How to Waste $100 Billion: Weapons That Didn't Work Out," *Forbes*, December 19, 2011.

For Further Discussion

Chapter 1

1. Carla Fried insists that the United States must make lowering its budget deficit a number one priority to prevent economic disaster. Economist Joseph E. Stiglitz contends that the opposite is true, and that the best way to help the economy is by lowering health care costs, raising tax revenue collected from corporations by getting rid of the loopholes used to avoid paying taxes, and creating jobs. Which author do you think provides better evidence to back up his or her claims? Where do you think the deficit should rank on America's list of economic priorities? Why?

2. Dean Baker advocates government intervention in the form of stimulus spending, lowering interest rates, and lowering the value of a dollar to create jobs and grow the economy. Peter D. Schiff argues that the economy will flourish if what he characterizes as government impediments to growth—regulations and spending on things like infrastructure and long-term unemployment benefits—are sharply reduced. What level of government intervention seems appropriate to deal with the deficit? Would it be possible to come up with a plan that combines aspects of these two approaches to deficit reduction? If so, what would that involve?

Chapter 2

1. Robert Reich says that the wealthy have been earning more during the last three decades and paying lower and lower taxes, while just the opposite has been true for working-class Americans. Raising the wealthy's taxes, he insists, will generate much-needed revenue without further burdening an already overtaxed middle class. Robert Frank

cautions against depending too greatly on tax revenue from the wealthy, because the nature of their earnings is dependent on the stock market, which is volatile and unreliable. Frank refers mostly to state tax revenues, while Reich emphasizes federal taxes. Do states seem more vulnerable to lost revenue than the federal government? Why or why not? Does Frank seem to indicate that increasing taxes on the wealthy at the federal level would be as precarious as raising them at the state level? Explain.

2. President Barack Obama says that the tax code must be reformed to better serve the American people and reduce the deficit, partly by raising tax revenue on the highest earners, who he says are taxed too lightly. Len Burman, although he differs on the type of reform that is needed, agrees with Obama that tax reform is an important goal. Nevertheless, Burman claims, unlike in the past, bipartisan support for reform is impossible to achieve. He says that Obama is so hated by Republicans who are trying to prevent him from being reelected that he has no chance of gaining the needed support. Do you agree with Burman's assessment of the political climate? Why or why not? Does President Obama's proposal seem reasonable? Why or why not?

Chapter 3

1. In her viewpoint, Michele Swenson says that political conservatives use the term "entitlement" in a derogatory sense, implying that those who receive federal assistance are expecting something to which they are not really entitled. She argues that "entitlement" is a more apt description of presumptuous, corrupt speculators who she says are rewarded for their unscrupulous activities that unload toxic assets at the expense of individual mortgage holders.

Do you think that the definition of entitlement affects the debate over spending on social programs? If so, how? If not, why not?

2. Alan S. Blinder says in his viewpoint that the cost of health care is the biggest driver of the deficit. Charles Blahous says it is the aging baby boom generation that is driving up costs. Which of their arguments did you find more convincing? Why? Do their main concerns overlap? If so, how? If not, why not?

Chapter 4

1. Do you believe the military budget is the right size or should it be cut? Read the viewpoints by David Morris and Robert J. Samuelson for opinions on both sides of the issue to inform your answer.

2. In the viewpoints by Taylor Marvin and Lawrence J. Korb, Laura Conley, and Alex Rothman, history is used as a means of illustrating what is possible and necessary with regard to modern-day spending on defense. Is looking at history a beneficial way to approach current policy and budget decisions? Why or why not?

Organizations to Contact

The editors have compiled the following list of organizations concerned with the issues debated in this book. The descriptions are derived from materials provided by the organizations. All have publications or information available for interested readers. The list was compiled on the date of publication of the present volume; the information provided here may change. Be aware that many organizations take several weeks or longer to respond to inquiries, so allow as much time as possible.

AARP
601 E Street NW, Washington, DC   20049
888-687-2277
e-mail: member@aarp.org
website: www.aarp.org

AARP, formerly known as the American Association of Retired Persons, is a nonprofit, nonpartisan organization with more than thirty million members and is the largest advocacy group of Americans over the age of fifty. It seeks to improve every aspect of living for older people and focuses on concerns such as health care and pensions. AARP is committed to preserving the federal Social Security and Medicare programs. The association publishes the monthly newsletter *AARP News Bulletin*, the bimonthly newsletter *Working Age*, and the bimonthly magazine *Modern Maturity*.

Americans for Prosperity (AFP)
2111 Wilson Boulevard, Suite 350, Arlington, VA   22201
888-730-0150
e-mail: info@AFPhq.org
website: http://americansforprosperity.org

Americans for Prosperity (AFP) is committed to educating citizens about economic policy and mobilizing those citizens as advocates in the public policy process. AFP is an organization of grassroots leaders who engage citizens in the name of limited government and free markets on the local, state, and federal levels. AFP supports cutting taxes and government spending in order to limit government's involvement in the economic lives of citizens; limiting tax and expenditure to promote fiscal responsibility; facilitating entrepreneurship and economic opportunity by involving citizens and reducing red tape and bureaucracy; and restoring fairness to the US judicial system. The group's website has position statements on issues with which it is concerned and organizes events in the thirty-five states in which it has chapters.

Americans United for Change

PO Box 65321, Washington, DC   20035
(202) 470-6954
website: www.americansunitedforchange.org

Americans United for Change is working to mobilize a broad network of grassroots activists to hold public officials accountable and to make progress on issues such as increasing the minimum wage, allowing Medicare to directly negotiate lower prices for prescription drugs, preventing the privatization of Social Security, and improving access to affordable health care. The group runs national media campaigns and publishes a blog and press releases regarding issues with which it is concerned.

Bipartisan Policy Center (BPC)

1225 Eye Street NW, Suite 1000, Washington, DC   20005
(202) 204-2400 • fax: (202) 637-9220
website: bipartisaninfo@bipartisanpolicy.org

The Bipartisan Policy Center (BPC) advocates budget and policy solutions through rigorous analysis, reasoned negotiation, and respectful dialogue. Founded in 2007 by former Senate Majority Leaders Howard Baker, Tom Daschle, Bob Dole, and George J. Mitchell, BPC combines politically balanced policy making with strong, proactive advocacy and outreach. It actively promotes bipartisanship to address the key challenges facing the nation. Its policy solutions come from deliberations by former elected and appointed officials, business and labor leaders, and academics and advocates who represent both ends of the political spectrum. The center is focused on health care, energy, national and homeland security, transportation, and the economy. It prepares reports, research, staff papers, testimony, and workshop materials, all of which are available on the center's website.

Brookings Institution
1775 Massachusetts Avenue NW, Washington, DC   20036
(202) 797-6000
website: www.brookings.edu

The Brookings Institution is a public policy organization that emphasizes strengthening American democracy; supporting the economic and social welfare, security, and opportunity of all Americans; and securing a more open, safe, prosperous, and cooperative international system. The institution publishes various newsletters, including the *Economic Studies Bulletin*, as well as journals such as *Brookings Papers on Economic Activity* and books like *Using Taxes to Reform Health Insurance*.

Cato Institute
1000 Massachusetts Avenue NW, Washington, DC   20001
(202) 842-0200 • fax: (202) 842-3490
website: www.cato.org

The Cato Institute is a public policy research foundation that promotes limited government, individual liberty, free markets, and peace. In addition to research, it provides educational information and encourages greater involvement of citizens in public policy discussions. The institute publishes the *Cato Journal, Cato Policy Report, Tax & Budget Bulletin, Economic Development Bulletin*, and several other publications.

Center for Economic and Policy Research (CEPR)
1611 Connecticut Avenue NW, Suite 400
Washington, DC   20009

(202) 293-5380
website: www.cepr.net

The Center for Economic and Policy Research (CEPR) conducts professional research and public education programs to promote democratic debate on important economic and social issues. CEPR is committed to presenting issues in an accurate and understandable manner so that the public is better prepared to choose among the various policy options. CEPR asserts that an informed public should be able to choose policies that lead to improving quality of life, both for people within the United States and around the world.

Center on Budget and Policy Priorities
820 First Street NE, Suite 510, Washington, DC 20002
(202) 408-1080 • fax: (202) 408-1056
e-mail: center@cbpp.org
website: www.cbpp.org

The Center on Budget and Policy Priorities focuses on fiscal policy at the state and federal levels and on public programs that affect low- and moderate-income families and individuals. The center conducts research and analysis to help shape public debates over proposed budget and tax policies, and it develops policy options to alleviate poverty. It publishes reports, blog posts, and press releases on issues with which it is concerned.

Citizens Against Government Waste (CAGW)
1301 Pennsylvania Avenue NW, Suite 1075
Washington, DC 20004
(202) 467-5300 • fax: (202) 467-4253
e-mail: membership@cagw.org
website www.cagw.org

Citizens Against Government Waste (CAGW) is a private, nonpartisan, nonprofit organization representing more than one million members and supporters nationwide. Founded in 1984, CAGW's mission is to eliminate waste, mismanagement, and inefficiency in the federal government. CAGW produces numerous publications highlighting wasteful government spending. *Government Waste Watch* is the group's quarterly newspaper, which is distributed to members of CAGW, Congress, and members of the media nationwide. CAGW's annual *Congressional Pig Book Summary* exposes the most glaring and irresponsible pork-barrel projects in annual appropriations bills.

Committee on the Budget, US House of Representatives
207 Cannon House Office Building, Washington, DC 20515
(202) 226-7270
website: http://budget.house.gov

According to the rules of the House of Representatives, the House Budget Committee is responsible for the "establishment, extension, and enforcement of special controls over the federal budget, including the budgetary treatment of off-budget federal agencies." The website includes pages with frequently asked questions about the budget process, laws governing the budgeting process, and current budget statistics.

Concord Coalition
1011 Arlington Boulevard, Suite 300, Arlington, VA 22209
(703) 894-6222 • fax: (703) 849-6231
website: www.concordcoalition.org

The Concord Coalition is a nonpartisan grassroots organization that seeks to educate the public about the causes and consequences of deficit spending on the part of the federal government. Subjects covered include the debt, the federal budget, Medicare and health care, Social Security, and tax entitlements.

Congressional Budget Office
Ford House Office Building, 4th Floor
Second and D Streets SW, Washington, DC 20515-6925
(202) 226-2600
website: www.cbo.gov

The Congressional Budget Office (CBO) mandate is to provide objective and timely analysis of budget proposals to the House and Senate Budget Committees and to members of the legislature to support the legislative process. The CBO website posts analyses of the economic impact of virtually every spending proposal considered by the legislature. Recent publications address the long-term budget outlook, the impact of health insurance policy on labor markets, and the economic costs of taxing carbon dioxide emissions.

Demos
220 Fifth Avenue, 2nd Floor, New York, NY   10001
(212) 633-1405
website: www.demos.org

Demos is a nonpartisan, public policy research and advocacy organization that works with advocates and policy makers around the country in pursuit of four overarching goals: a more equitable economy with widely shared prosperity and opportunity; a vibrant and inclusive democracy with high levels of voting and civic engagement; an empowered public sector that works for the common good; and responsible US engagement in an interdependent world.

Heritage Foundation
214 Massachusetts Avenue NE, Washington, DC   20002-4999
(202) 546-4400
website: www.heritage.org

The Heritage Foundation is a research and educational organization whose mission is to formulate and promote conservative public policies based on the principles of free enterprise, limited government, individual freedom, traditional American values, and a strong national defense.

Moment of Truth Project
1899 L Street NW, Suite 400, Washington, DC   20003
(202) 596-3431 • fax: (202) 986-3696
website: www.momentoftruthproject.org

The Moment of Truth Project aims to use the fiscal commission's findings to spark a national discussion on the need to implement a comprehensive budget fix and to help further develop the policy reform ideas to improve the nation's fiscal outlook. The Moment of Truth Project is an initiative of the Committee for a Responsible Federal Budget, a bipartisan, nonprofit organization committed to educating the public about issues that have significant fiscal policy impact. It publishes policy papers, op-ed pieces, and press releases, all of which are available on its website.

National Priorities Project (NPP)
243 King Street, Suite 109, Northampton, MA   01060
(413) 584-9556
website: http://nationalpriorities.org

The National Priorities Project (NPP) works to explain the complex federal budget in a way that is accessible, allowing people to exercise their right and responsibility to oversee and influence how their tax dollars are spent. NPP works for an effective and accountable federal government that promotes the general welfare of the nation. NPP believes the US federal budget will reflect the values and priorities of the majority of Americans when all people have the opportunity and ability to participate in shaping the nation's budget. On its website, NPP provides training information on budget basics, access to webinars, and a tool kit for educators.

OMB Watch
1742 Connecticut Avenue NW, Washington, DC   20009
(202) 234-8494 • fax: (202) 234-8584
website: http://ombwatch.org

OMB Watch, a nonprofit research and advocacy organization, was formed in 1983 to explain the role of the White House Office of Management and Budget (OMB). The OMB oversees federal regulation, the budget, information collection and dissemination, proposed legislation, testimony by agencies, and much more. Since its founding, OMB Watch has expanded its focus to address substantive issues, including the federal budget, taxation, government performance, nonprofit speech and advocacy rights, and regulatory policy. It publishes articles and analysis, as well as a blog, all of which can be found on its website.

Public Agenda

6 East Thirty-Ninth Street, 9th Floor, New York, NY 10016
(212) 686-6610
website: www.publicagenda.org/

Public Agenda is a nonpartisan, nonprofit public policy research and education organization that seeks to bridge the gap between American leaders and what the public really thinks about issues ranging from education to foreign policy to immigration to religion and civility in American life. It does this by helping American leaders better understand the public's point of view and by helping citizens know more about critical policy issues so they can make thoughtful, informed decisions.

US Senate Budget Committee

624 Dirksen Senate Office Building, Washington, DC 20510
(202) 224-0642
website: http://budget.senate.gov

Along with the House Budget Committee, the Senate Budget Committee is responsible for drafting Congress's annual budget plan and monitoring action on the budget for the federal government. The Senate Budget Committee's website links to separate resources on the budget, posted by Republican and Democratic senators.

Bibliography of Books

Bruce Bartlett   *The Benefit and the Burden: Tax Reform—Why We Need It and What It Will Take.* New York: Simon & Schuster, 2012.

Scott Bittle and   *Where Does the Money Go?: Your Guided Tour to the Federal Budget Crisis.* New York: Harper, 2011.
Jean Johnson

Tom Blair   *Poorer Richard's America: What Would Ben Say?* New York: Skyhorse Pub., 2010.

Peter A. Diamond   *Saving Social Security: A Balanced Approach.* Washington, DC: Brookings Institution Press, 2005.
and Peter R.
Orszag

Robert Eisner   *The Great Deficit Scares: The Federal Budget, Trade, and Social Security.* New York: Century Foundation Press, 1997.

Robert Eisner   *How Real Is the Federal Deficit?* New York: Free Press, 1986.

Peter Ferrara   *America's Ticking Bankruptcy Bomb: How the Looming Debt Crisis Threatens the American Dream—and How We Can Turn the Tide Before It's Too Late.* New York: Broadside Books, 2011.

Ellen Frank   *The Raw Deal: How Myths and*
                     Misinformation About Deficits,
                     Inflation, and Wealth Impoverish
                     America. Boston, MA: Beacon Press,
                     2004.

Richard Heinberg   *The End of Growth: Adapting to Our*
                     New Economic Reality. Gabriola
                     Island, British Columbia: New
                     Society Publishers, 2011.

Richard A. Iley   *Untangling the US Deficit: Evaluating*
and Mervyn K.   *Causes, Cures and Global Imbalances.*
Lewis   Northampton, MA: Edward Elgar,
                     2007.

Sophia R. Ketler,   *Medicaid: Services, Costs and Future.*
ed.   New York: Nova Science, 2008.

Paul Krugman   *End This Depression Now!* New York:
                     W.W. Norton, 2012.

Paul Krugman   *The Great Unraveling: Losing Our*
                     Way in the New Century. New York:
                     W.W. Norton, 2004.

Michael Moran   *The Reckoning: Debt, Democracy, and*
                     the Future of American Power. New
                     York: Palgrave Macmillan, 2012.

Iwan Morgan   *The Age of Deficits: Presidents and*
                     Unbalanced Budgets from Jimmy
                     Carter to George W. Bush. Lawrence:
                     University Press of Kansas, 2009.

Peter G. Peterson *Running on Empty: How the Democratic and Republican Parties Are Bankrupting Our Future and What Americans Can Do About It.* New York: Farrar, Straus and Giroux, 2004.

Alice M. Rivlin and Isabel Sawhill, eds. *Restoring Fiscal Sanity, 2005: Meeting the Long-Run Challenge.* Washington, DC: Brookings Institution Press, 2005.

Michael Savage *Trickle Down Tyranny: Crushing Obama's Dream of the Socialist States of America.* New York: William Morrow, 2012.

Allen Schick *The Federal Budget: Politics, Policy, Process.* 3rd ed. Washington, DC: Brookings Institution Press, 2007.

Vanessa C. Sibhoan, ed. *From Surplus to Deficit: The Impact of Legislation on the Federal Budget.* Hauppauge, NY: Nova Science Publishers, 2011.

Joseph E. Stiglitz *Freefall: America, Free Markets, and the Sinking of the World Economy.* New York: W.W. Norton, 2010.

Joseph E. Stiglitz, Amartya Sen, and Jean-Paul Fitoussi *Mis-Measuring Our Lives: Why GDP Doesn't Add Up.* New York: The New Press, 2010.

Martin A. Sullivan *Corporate Tax Reform: Taxing Profits in the 21st Century.* New York: Apress, 2011.

Timothy Taylor   *The Instant Economist: Everything You Need to Know About How the Economy Works.* New York: Plume, 2012.

Richard E. Wagner   *Deficits, Debt, and Democracy: Wrestling with Tragedy on the Fiscal Commons.* Northampton, MA: Edward Elgar, 2012.

Winslow T. Wheeler, ed.   *America's Defense Meltdown: Pentagon Reform for President Obama and the New Congress.* Stanford, CA: Stanford University Press, 2009.

Addison Wiggin and Kate Incontrera   *I.O.U.S.A.* Hoboken, NJ: Wiley, 2008.

Andrew L. Yarrow   *Forgive Us Our Debts: The Intergenerational Dangers of Fiscal Irresponsibility.* New Haven, CT: Yale University Press, 2008.

Index

A

B

I

J